# OLD AMERICAN HOUSES
*And How to Restore Them*

[1700–1850]

# OLD AMERICAN HOUSES

## And *How to Restore Them*

[1700–1850]

*by*

HENRY LIONEL WILLIAMS

*and*

OTTALIE K. WILLIAMS

DOUBLEDAY & COMPANY, INC.

*Garden City, New York*

1946

*To All Who Love Old Houses*

# Credo

*We believe:*

That it is quite possible to create a modern, up-to-date home in a small house belonging to another age, blending with the quiet simplicity of old-time living the advantages of present-day labor-saving facilities, materials, and methods.

That living in an old-time house does not necessarily connote an old-fashioned way of life, with its accompaniments of drudgery and dirt. And it does offer something besides the hard impersonality of plate glass, the clinical asepsis of white enamel, the cacophony of clanging tin cupboards, and hard lines that make a fetish of function at the price of restful beauty and elevate the machine product above the manual skills of the craftsman who put something of himself in everything he made.

That in this feverish age, when change is so often mistaken for progress, we would all do well to consider the advantages of a lessened tempo in our hours of relaxation. A less challenging atmosphere than that which the modernists offer is a step in the right direction. In our small towns, villages, and rural countrysides we can still find these quiet backwaters: small worlds where harried human existence gives way to more natural living, and people have time to be neighbors instead of competitors in an economic race. There the quiet, unostentatious small house is the symbol and the core of a way of life that is human—a far cry from the materialistic impersonality of the modern functional cage that is the dream of those who forget that sentiment is as important as reason in a full and rounded life.

# Preface

THE buying of a little old house to make into a home is, for the understanding, a sentimental adventure that can bring rich rewards. But to achieve the aim of making it livable, in the twentieth-century sense, without destroying its character and rubbing off the mellow bloom of age, calls for far more knowledge and determination than we may realize at first. More often than not, this job of intelligent remodeling is coupled with the need for removing the mistakes of others and restoring features that have been altered or eliminated by those who did not value the things that give these early houses their distinctive charm. Both of these matters require attention soon after the house is bought. The process of acquiring a house is, therefore, not the end but the beginning of a venture that may bring years of satisfaction and happiness, or disappointment and regrets. The decision lies in the manner in which the restoration and adaptations are carried out. These are matters in which most people need help, for intelligence is no valid substitute for experience, and enthusiasm is no sure guide.

The purpose of this book is to answer some of the questions which every new owner of an old house must sometime ask; to reveal the skill and care which our forefathers put into the little houses that became the first American homes; and to show how their character, developed and sometimes marred by time and human activity, can be preserved or revived.

If you are one of those who seek, but have not yet found, one of these small houses built a century and a half or two centuries ago, there is encouragement in knowing how much can be done to re-

# Preface

capture the spirit of the past and make it a splendid part of life today. Even in the searching there are compensations for the time and effort spent.

As we discovered long ago, prospecting for an old-time house can be as thrilling as a treasure hunt, and more worth while. As you drive along quiet village streets, through tangled lanes and over hilltop trails, or wade through hog wallows and farmyard mud in search of a house, you are likely to acquire a good deal more than an appetite and muddy shoes. And you will be amazed at the quaint notions of owners and brokers as to what constitutes "a desirable old house with original features and old-fashioned charm."

In your journeyings you will stumble across weird examples of the "restoration" and remodeling of ancient architectural gems. And you will discover lonely old houses rotting away for the want of a little care—for the need of someone with imagination enough to see the possibilities beneath the incipient decay.

These things we know from long experience, first in one part of the country and then another as fate decided we should relocate our home. In scorching summer, white-smothered winter, and melting spring we have spent long and sometimes cheerless days in search of an un-spoiled yet livable eighteenth-century country home. And each time our persistence was rewarded. When we found our latest treasure it was midwinter, with heavy snow upon the ground, piled window-high. Yet, as we soon discovered, dull day or bright, the house lost none of its appeal, and even the bedraggled and neglected garden and the ice-filled gutters could not detract from its simple charm.

That is the lure of this hunt in all season. Turning a corner or topping a rise, you never know what lies just beyond; at what angle or in what mood you will strike the house you have come to see.

And so, if in the end you are fortunate enough to come into possession of an old-time house, think well before you begin to tear it apart. Irreparable damage can be wrought if such things are done in haste. If no competent architect is at hand to advise, the knowledge of how to go about restoring and remodeling properly and sympathetically

# Preface

can be acquired with little effort by anyone who can read. And there are generally local antiquarian societies ready and willing to help.

In our searches for potential homes for ourselves and for our friends who, knowing of our interest in such things, have solicited our help, we have found the answers to many problems that face the owners of an old-time house. For the rest of the facts and suggestions embalmed within these pages we have to thank those many friends who have opened their houses for us to explore, photograph, and sketch; our good friends and neighbors: J. Theodore Rogers, surveyor and antiquarian; Edward F. Plumb, who brought so many lovely relics to our attention; and John Ward, cabinetmaker extraordinary, who introduced us to the delights of old woods and finishes; to Elizabeth W. Morrison, Assistant Librarian of the Springfield, Massachusetts, City Library, for her indefatigable aid in research; to Carl W. Drepperd for his invaluable suggestions; and to the authors of books on all phases of the subject, mentioned in the bibliographical list, against whose experiences we have checked our own, and on whom we have drawn for information not available elsewhere.

OTTALIE AND LIONEL WILLIAMS

Sherman, Connecticut
May 1946

[ 9 ]

# Contents

# Contents

# Contents

# Illustrations

# Illustrations

# Illustrations

## HALF TONES

# Illustrations

# INTRODUCTION

# Understanding Old Houses

A GREAT many people love old houses, but few really understand them. Just as so many "know nothing about art but know what they like when they see it," so do the majority of those who go into ecstasies over eighteenth-century cottages respond to their emotions rather than their intellect. And emotion—that ebullience of feeling compounded of the thrill of discovery and elation over possession—is no safe foundation for the conversion of an old-time house into a home.

A feeling for old houses, like an artistic temperament, is something you are born with—or without. It can be encouraged or repressed, but it cannot be created. To the average person there is nothing more appealing than a quaint old house nestling among ancient trees and hugging the ground from which it seems to have sprung. Yet, in the majority of cases, these selfsame people would hesitate to buy one of these very old houses to live in. It seems that there are more practical-minded people than dreamers among us, and most of us who pride ourselves on our practicality are lacking in the vision necessary mentally to picture such a house as a home possessing all the attributes and conveniences required for modern, comfortable living. That is why a feeling for the ancient house is no indication that we are capable of converting it into a satisfactory home. Something else is needed, and that something is understanding.

Understanding comes only from study and thought. We often like things we do not fully appreciate because we do not go beyond first impressions, and, if we did, we would not know what to look for in them. In small, old-time houses, for example, we generally seek that aura or atmosphere that we vaguely label "charm." But recognizing charm and analyzing it are two different breeds of cat. Yet, in making over an old house, our aim must be to preserve that charm—something that we cannot deliberately do unless we know exactly what that charm consists of in the first place!

One of the chief components of charm, it seems to us, is character. Fortunately character is independent of style or period, though general appearance has a great deal to do with it. We have in mind one perfectly charming house that we know which is simply plastered with early Victorian gingerbread. This house, which normally would be considered an atrocity, is painted dead white all over, with a roof of light gray slate, and it nestles in the fold of a hill covered with big trees. This treatment and the setting have turned something grotesque into a house, perky and proud, like a fairy castle, a delight to the eye.

The first impression that you get of a house is the result of an automatic, often unconscious, mental appraisal of its outstanding features —its proportions, lines, balance, texture (surface), and color, and the way it fits into its background. But none of these is of much importance, in an old-time house, without that lived-in quality—a feeling of domesticity. After all, what we seek in an old house is something that no new house can give us; something that the much overworked word "charm" covers but does not define.

Both use and age add something that nothing else can supply, and that is character. New things like houses and furniture can have beauty, but only old, well-used ones have character. This character cannot be created in a house any more than it can in a person. It is acquired through the treatment it receives over a long period of time. Like old furniture, houses gain character from being lived with, and personality from the marks that time, weathering, and human handling have left upon them.

This is why, when you buy an old house, you acquire something more than a collection of time-worn lumber and moss-covered shingles. You have something that has been a part of people's lives for generations; something that has meant a great deal to those who have lived in it and cared for it and left their human imprint on it. And, above all, if you have chosen aright, you have a house that has

# Introduction

weathered well the storms of a century or two, and is good for centuries more. For this reason, to those who appreciate these things, no new house can have the charm or appeal of an old one.

Old houses, then, are like oysters. If you like them, you love them; if you don't, you detest them, and people who go wild over them seem lacking in sense. Yet many a person or family that has not developed a taste for houses built a century or more ago has come to learn that what such houses lack in modernity they gain in character and comfort. For the rest—people who do not like old houses should not buy them. But, alas, they do!

It is one of the misfortunes of our time that such people not only buy old-time houses but sink quantities of cold, hard cash into making them over into "cute" nondescripts that have all the air of venerable old ladies in theatrical make-up and tights! We recall, only too well, a little pre-Revolutionary stone house that we looked at ever so long ago; eight tiny rooms on three floors, and one of the beautiful stone fireplaces converted into a whitewashed brick bar, while the old plastered walls were covered with modern murals in oil of scenes from the zoo!

It seems to us that there are three kinds of people who acquire old houses: those who want something low in cost, or ready-made, to turn into a modern dwelling; those who like the idea of living in an old house but don't quite know why; and those who seek the satisfactions of a house that has seen a lot of living, and who appreciate the craftsmanship and honest labor and materials that went into its building.

For the first of these the house is but an agglomeration of building materials. This book is not for them. For those of the second group, perhaps all that is needed is a little thought and a guiding hand. For them, this "inside story" of old houses that have been cherished homes for a hundred years or more may be the spark that kindles understanding and appreciation.

Those who know that old houses have personalities derived from the living and the loving, the borning and the dying, the reunions and leave-takings that have gone on, generation after generation, within their walls; whose worn doorsteps and shining baluster rails bear mute witness to the myriad comings and goings of children, and of old people now long dead—these need no telling of the comforting feeling of continuity, the endless flow of life concentrated in and permeating the place that now shelters them. Nor do they need to be told of the necessity for preserving the atmosphere, the feeling of belonging, even in modifying the structure, as too often we are compelled to do.

These are the people who buy century-old houses because they want an old house with all its old-time charm and atmosphere. And they buy more of such houses in the country because there are more of them there to be had. So many of the town houses of the old days have been demolished to make way for more up-to-date buildings during the past fifty years or so. But whether it is a town house or a country house, the idea is the same: to preserve as much as possible of what we have, while adapting the place to present-day needs. The only practical way to go about this is to plan carefully every step. But you cannot even begin to do that till you are thoroughly familiar with the house, its history, layout, and construction.

Houses, like people, change with age, and not always for the better. Throughout the United States there are very many houses that were built between the end of the seventeenth century and the beginning of the eighteen hundreds—houses that still have left to them many of the original features that gave them their charm and made them a delight to the eye. But far many more of those that survive have succumbed to whim, taste, or fashion through the long years of their life.

In the 1870s many a fine old Colonial was dressed up with a mansard roof like a self-conscious laborer in a top hat, or given a durable coating of stucco (we once lived in one that had both!). In the drab nineties, little-paned windows became old-fashioned (as if that were a crime). Single or double-light sashes were substituted for the old six-over-sixes or twelve-over-nines.

In that ghastly era the old doors, too, subject to so much wear and tear, were ruthlessly torn out and thrown away or used for kindling fires in the chunk stoves that cluttered up the hearths. Smart modern

# Introduction

oak ones with heavily molded panels or gothic lights became the rage. With the days of increased leisure and a keener interest in the neighbors came an epidemic of porches, sometimes around three sides of the house. Because of the light shut out by these abominations, and the heavy Victorian drapes, bigger windows were installed, often of the french type opening to the floor! Blessings upon the old-house owner who, through these vacillations of taste and fashion, clung to the old and tried, and declared that what was good enough for great-grandfather was good enough for him!

Now the wheel of fashion in old-time houses has turned its full cycle again. People have learned to appreciate the good and beautiful in domestic architecture, and reject the dogma of the Philistine that what is new is best. Porches are being torn off houses from Maine to Minnesota; small-paned windows are ousting the blank and characterless stares of single, large lights. Cellars and barns are being scoured for the original doors, and the old-time handmade hardware that the junk snupper has not yet purloined.

But, we must confess, in far too many instances misguided enthusiasm is making changes for the worse. Imitation hinge straps, outside and in, mar fine old doors; hammer marks, carefully applied to ironwork, emphasize its pseudo-authenticity to those who know better. Indoor hardware is painted black to insure that its old-fashioned form does not escape the eye of the admiring visitor. Knotty pine, the knottier the better, so beloved of the uninformed "paneled"-wall addict, would make the old-time carpenter sick.

These and a thousand other crimes against taste and authenticity are committed daily by the unknowing, and the amateur remodeler who seizes the form to miss the spirit, and thinks less of recapturing charm than of displaying his intimacy with things of an earlier day.

The end result of all this is houses that gain in "quaintness" and "cuteness" what they lose in venerable dignity and charm. What is more, they lose in cash value in the eyes of the informed buyer and the student of this vital cultural heritage bequeathed us by our forbears who built for the generations to come because that was the only way they knew how to build—honestly of honest materials, by men imbued with the pride of skilled craftsmanship.

As a rule, the only old houses in existence today that are worth putting in condition for modern living are those built in the East, between 1700 and 1830, and perhaps twenty years later beyond the Alleghenies, for these usually are the traditional houses of long ago when a man built with the idea of permanency—for himself and for his family for generations to come. Those built before 1700 that have not been remodeled are museum pieces and should be preserved as such. The same thing might be said of many built after that time, but such houses are not likely to fall into the hands of the casual buyer.

In these pages, therefore, we have not concerned ourselves with the unspoiled old houses built prior to 1700, or with the larger and more pretentious old Colonials of any style. Our interest has been confined to those modest small dwellings of the farmhouse type most frequently found in rural districts, small towns, and sometimes the suburbs of large ones. Year by year, these old Colonials which have endured the summer suns and winter snows for many generations grow fewer and fewer as fire, hurricane, neglect, termites, or sheer old age take their toll. The wonder is that there are any left at all!

Fortunately it is still possible to find antique houses that time and changing fashion have dealt with kindly; houses that have possessed owners with understanding, or even indifferent ones who have been content to leave well enough alone. Lucky is the buyer who is able to acquire such a treasure, and lucky is the house if he treats it with sympathy and care. With a little thought and a certain amount of knowledge, the charm and simplicity that gives an antique house its appeal may be retained, even while we adapt it to our needs.

And so if we must restore and remodel, or "modernize," at least let us do it right, preserving what is lent to us for our brief time for those who come after us to enjoy. It takes a century or more of care to preserve these old-time houses that cannot be replaced. Lack of knowledge and understanding in restoring and remodeling can spoil them in a day!

# OLD AMERICAN HOUSES

*And How to Restore Them*

[1700–1850]

# CHAPTER I

# The Old Colonial

AMERICANS have been building houses for more than four hundred years, but the fashioning of small dwellings that expressed the rising culture of the fledgling nation came to an end almost a hundred years ago. When steam sawmills began to spawn boards, planks, and scantlings by the million, the day of the individual housebuilder came to an end. With the arrival of the industrial age, the carpenter craftsman passed from the scene, housebuilding deteriorated from an art to a business, and something human and precious was lost.

While it is true that many a pioneer did design and build his own home, most of them were satisfied to call in a carpenter and leave to him the responsibility of interpreting their characters and aspirations in wood, brick, and stone. And surviving specimens of contracts show that they gave him plenty of leeway in his choice of style and decoration.

Early housebuilding on these shores was largely a matter of precedent and rule of thumb. The carpenter or mason who had learned his trade through long apprenticeship became the architect and followed closely the ideas drilled into him by the man who had taught him. Evolution was slow, but many of these men had ideas of their own that gave their work a distinctive touch which is particularly obvious when we compare exterior details. The interior of course was the thing that mattered most to the owner—and his wife; the shelter, the warmth, and the security. A substantial frame that no ordinary hurricane could demolish, a windproof wall, and a water-tight roof were prime considerations, which, alas, were seldom achieved. Ample fireplaces for heating and cooking came next. Light was the least problem, because the smaller the windows the less chance for heat to escape and intruders to enter. And, the price of glass being what it was, large windows were an extravagance.

That was in the beginning. Later, when the surviving Indians had been chased farther into the wilderness and a more prosperous day began to dawn, the old homestead commenced to seem less adequate. Things that formerly were luxuries, such as ample daylight in every room, became necessities. The heavy and forbidding door, designed to exclude scalp-hunting redskins, tax collectors, and blizzards, gave way to more friendly portals that beckoned the visitor inside. Like a gold Prince Albert across a Victorian waistcoat, it was the focal point of the front that gave the whole structure importance.

In growing communities, visiting grew more common, and the womenfolk had greater opportunities to appraise and compare. The house became a more important index of the social standing and attitudes of those it sheltered. The carpenter was called upon to dress it up and make it look more important than it was.

And so developed the typical American small house of the eighteenth century that remains to us as a splendid cultural heritage that not all of us appreciate as we should. Not to the house owners so much as to the old-time carpenters and masons do we owe the lovely old houses of a century to two and a half centuries ago that we so eagerly take to our bosoms today—sometimes to their benefit, too often to their detriment. Like ardent lovers we seize upon these heirlooms to make them more wholly ours by "molding them nearer to the heart's desire." This is the temptation we have to brace ourselves to resist; the sin against which we must steel our hearts.

In few other human relationships—and who can say that a house that has been lived in for two hundred years is not at least partly human?—is it more necessary to know what we are doing before we do it. Houses, like people, grow and evolve with the slow passing of time, and time is a part of nature that can do wonderful and lovely things to the creations of mankind if we let it. The tragedy is that these things can be so quickly undone by a moment's thoughtlessness, indifference, or ignorance, and since the end is the same, who is to say which is worst?

Architects who love to point to the growth of the national character as revealed by its houses may scoff at this. And we are ready to compromise by admitting that what they claim may be true in the case of the larger and more pretentious houses which architects have designed and which have since been left pretty much alone. Just as painters interpret their times in their art, so do architects interpret them in three-dimensional materials and structures. But here we are concerned with the *small* house in which the architect was, for the most part, replaced by the carpenter, and the artist by the artisan. Because of this, the small houses are really more representative of the people than are the larger houses and mansions that serve to display the wealth and position of the gentry and merchant princes.

These small houses, of which there are so many scattered all over the land, are the kind and size of house that the average American family of today can live in and afford to buy and maintain. And they are all *old* houses—very old, measured by the time that has elapsed since the first Anglo-Saxon set foot on Virginia's shore with a firm intention of making that his home. These were the houses that were built in the days when the colonies flourished, and whose erection continued till long after the peace trumpets had sounded for the close of Mr. Madison's war and the great western trek had begun.

Before settling down to a critical discussion of these houses, it may be as well to clear the ground by defining the styles of houses with which we shall have to deal. This, unfortunately, will not be so simple a process as it may sound. Dates are specific things, definite and unequivocal. And ancient houses too often seem more loath to reveal their year of origin than any coy lady on the downhill side of forty. Equally vague are the pretensions of many a house to some single style of architecture, and many defy almost any narrow classification. Yet there are some useful rules and principles we can follow. And if we cannot clear up *all* of these mysteries, at least we can lay some fallacies as we trace the history of the American house from 1700 to 1850.

No other art has suffered so much at the hands of its friends as the architecture of early America. Time and again attempts have been made to simplify the subject for the benefit of the layman, with disastrous results. Equal confusion is found in works intended for professional use, where existing features of houses have been carefully reproduced, but much less care taken in authenticating their dates. Fiske Kimball gives one very illuminating example when he points out that the exterior of the much-photographed Bergen house on Long Island, which is supposed to represent a Dutch type of 1655, was considerably altered in 1819, and many features belong to 1824.

This is the thing we are faced with in studying almost any old house: What changes have been made in it through the centuries, and when? In too many instances these questions are impossible of answer, and we have to rely on deduction and analogy. Where a house of a known date has special features, it is logical to assume that other houses, particularly in that same general locality, can be dated from the fact that they have those same features. But even there logic can only suggest; it cannot confirm, and all we are left with is a shrewd guess at the best.

In the minds of a great many of us, any old-time house that is not definitely Victorian—a style characterized by a profusion of gables, porches, and fretwork—is automatically classed as Old Colonial. The word "Old" merely serves to distinguish these houses from modern reproductions of the same styles.

At the other end of the scale of technical knowledge, the architect casts a severe eye on this indiscriminate grouping of a variety of styles which the trained eye can so readily distinguish. It is, of course, highly probable that no one who buys a small house built between 1700 and 1850—the period limits we have set ourselves—will acquire an unspoiled or pure example of any one architectural style. And in the majority of cases this does not matter overmuch. But there are certain fundamental features by which the various kinds of houses are differentiated, and architectural style is one of them. It may therefore be as well to consider what these styles were and how they originated.

Logically, any house built before 1783, when the colonies ceased to exist as such, could be called a Colonial. But since the same type of construction, workmanship, and architectural features were incorporated in houses built as late as the early eighteen hundreds, there is no reason why such later houses should not also be considered Colonials. These so-called Colonials, however, were far from being all alike. Some were of brick or stone, others of wood, or combinations of all three. Some had one kind of floor plan, some another, but the most striking differences were in the external appearance as dictated by the location of the chimney or chimneys, and the consequent arrangement of doors, windows, and other structural features.

The first of the Colonials, being strictly utilitarian, were extremely simple in design and appearance, and ranged from one to two and a half stories high. Foursquare and forthright, they relied on the proportions of walls and roof, and the placement and sizes of windows (technically known as fenestration) and doors for their architectural character. While they were originally copied from English and European styles, they had been modified to suit the climate and materials available in the New World. In the northeastern colonies, these houses were generally of wood, with the rooms grouped around a central chimney. In the southern colonies they were more often of brick, with chimneys at each end. These were the first real Colonials. But, since there were later types of Colonials, these original ones are generally referred to as Early American to distinguish them from the styles that developed later.

These Early American houses were built throughout the entire period with which we are concerned, and the style is therefore of little value as an indication of the age of any particular house. For that we have to rely on the constructional details, concerning which we shall have much to say a little later on.

In the 1720s, builders of the larger American houses—usually carpenters or masons, since there were no professional architects here then

—began to copy or adapt ideas from the more classic style then developing in England. This style is called Georgian because it blossomed during the reigns of the first English kings named George. The builders of small houses were quick to adopt the various decorative devices used on the larger houses, and the Early American began to lose some of its simple charm. The change was not always for the better

Georgian doorways were more
imposing.

because, while a carpenter might copy some Georgian detail, he rarely could resist adding some quirk of his own. Some of them, like true artists, interpreted instead of copying, but when they did not understand the principles involved, they often made ludicrous mistakes.

The Georgian house had a chimney at each end, sometimes two. Doorways were more imposing, and windows emphasized by the addition of pediments, decorated brick arches, or stone lintels. Bold moldings or other decorations such as dentils were used under eaves;

# The Old Colonial

rafter feet were extended and boxed in; facia boards were adorned with garlands or festoons; and eaves, supported by heavy cornices, extended beyond the gable ends. The social aims of the owners and the enthusiasm of the carpenters generally determined the lengths to which these embellishments were added and the Georgian style copied. The result was a great variety and degree of modified styles and the erection of many houses that were neither Early American nor Georgian but a little of both.

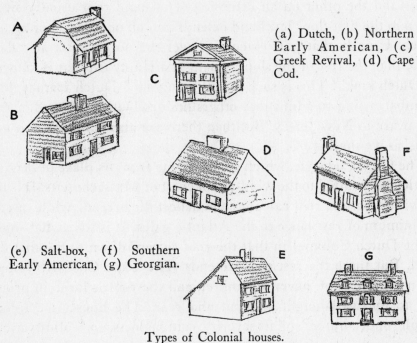

(a) Dutch, (b) Northern Early American, (c) Greek Revival, (d) Cape Cod.

(e) Salt-box, (f) Southern Early American, (g) Georgian.

Types of Colonial houses.

This gradual metamorphosis went on till the late 1790s, when Thomas Jefferson revived the long-neglected classic style of ancient Rome. This Romanesque style quickly gave way to an even more severely classical one that aimed at turning every house into a miniature Greek temple, with columns, pedimented gables, and elaborate friezes. The smaller house contracted this infection, and in the 1820s a rash of Greek Revival eight-, ten-, and twelve-room houses appeared, turning villages and towns into caricatures of the Athenian Acropolis.

[ 33 ]

# Old American Houses

These, then, are the three major architectural styles which left their mark upon the small Colonial house. There are, however, a number of important subdivisions or variations that frequently crop up to confound the layman and puzzle the expert. Three of these are the Dutch Colonial, Cape Cod, and the salt-box.

The distinguishing feature of the Dutch Colonial is not, as so many think, a gambrel roof. The Dutch type of house may have a gambrel roof or a plain pitched roof, and very often has both—one on the main house and the other on an extension. The main roof usually sweeps down to the first-floor level and extends out, on one side, over an open porch. Usually that part extending over the porch is set at a flatter angle than the rest of the slope, giving it a jaunty tilt that is known as a "Dutch kick"! This is such a well-recognized Dutch feature that it is embarrassing to admit that others besides Dutchmen used it, from Delaware to New Jersey. But then there are also gambrels and gambrels, as we shall see.

The Cape Cod style, which gets its name from its place of origin, is particularly suited to the wind-swept coast of Massachusetts. It is low-set with a massive roof calculated to deflect the breezes, while offering a minimum of resistance to the Atlantic gales. It is somewhat similar to the Dutch Colonial in that the roof sweeps down to the first-floor level. But there the resemblance ends. The Cape Cod always has a plain pitched roof, never a gambrel, and the roof is large in proportion to the wall height at front and rear. The house is extremely simple, undecorated, and its severity, compactness, and solidity are the sources of its charm. Being never more than a story and a half high, there are no upstairs windows except in the gables. Dormers are absent in the pure Cape Cod. The large chimney is always in the center of the roof, and the main entrance centered in the front wall. Today a thousand variations of these features are found on so-called Cape Cod-style houses which have no valid claim to that name at all.

The salt-box, over which many otherwise placid persons go into ecstasies, is merely a two-story house one room deep, from back to front, to the rear of which a single-story lean-to has been added. This

results in a roof which comes down much lower at the back than it
does at the front, so that, from the end, the house seems shaped somewhat like an old-fashioned salt box. In the later years houses of this
style were deliberately built and did not merely evolve from something else. In such houses there is no visible line of demarcation between the main portion and the lean-to, either in the walls or roof.

It would be nice and cozy if we could catalog the various styles of
houses precisely, listing the exact features of each type and showing on
a map just where those types were to be found comfortably segregated
in specific areas. Unfortunately for us, our colonial forbears were
highly individualistic in some respects, and the type of house they
lived in was a matter to which numbers of them gave considerable
thought. Thus we find the New England type house in the South, and
southern Early Americans in the North. We discover compromises
between them—one end chimney instead of two; end chimneys combined with gambrel roofs and front-porch overhangs; chimneys built
into the gables and chimneys built outside the gables, and both kinds
in one house; Dutch stone houses with wide roof overhangs at both
sides, and so on, ad infinitum.

These many departures from the general trend, however, do not
alter the fact that the three basic types mentioned predominated, and
most houses built after 1700 were of these types or recognizable variations of them.

As a result, wherever you find one of these old houses you will ordinarily have no difficulty in identifying it, in spite of the fact that
houses built in different parts of the country often vary in detail and in
the materials used. The constructional features were often influenced
by climatic conditions, the materials with which the local builder had
to work, the date of the settlement of that particular section, and so on,
as well as the economic and social standing of the men who footed the
bills. Houses built in Virginia and Maryland, for example, differ considerably from houses of the same style put up in New York or Ver-
mont, and New Jersey has many examples of a definitely local style.

The middle-western states of Michigan, Wisconsin, Indiana,

Illinois, and northern Ohio were settled, to a large extent, by New Englanders who built their houses in the style and manner to which they were accustomed in the particular section from which they came; so that we find the New England type of Early American house cropping up in these states. The same holds true of Kentucky, Tennessee, and southern Ohio, where we find houses of the Early American southern type of architecture, due to their early settlers having come over the Appalachians from the southern Atlantic seaboard states. In that part of Ohio still known as the Western Reserve may be found old farmhouses similar to those of Connecticut and Massachusetts—simple, braced-frame buildings, covered with clapboards, and frequently having an ell wandering off in the rear.

In the Middle West there are few old houses of the Georgian type. The reason for this is that by the time the immigrants had settled themselves and built their Early American houses, the Greek Revival came along, sweeping all before it. The late Georgian style, therefore, did not have time to make its influence felt.

These, then, are some of the factors that influenced the adoption of the three major architectural styles in various parts of the country. In addition, of course, there are many modifications introduced by the influx of settlers from France, Germany, Sweden, and other European countries, who brought along ideas of their own. Such variations from the general trend, however, are localisms superimposed on and often blended with the characteristic details of the typical early houses of the Early American, the Georgian, and the Greek Revival styles.

# CHAPTER II

# Hallmarks of Houses

## *The Northern Early American*

THE two principal prototypes of the Early American house are
that from the northeastern colonies and that common to the
warmer sections of the South. In the Northeast, from 1700 to almost
the middle of the nineteenth century, all-wood houses—which is what
most of them were—were built around a frame of sturdy timbers,
tenoned and pegged together, resting on substantial foundations of
stone or, more rarely, brick. In most cases there was a cellar under part
or all of the house, though usually it was not very deep.

The foundations, or underpinning, extended only a few inches above
the ground, and the siding came well down over it, giving the house
an appearance of hugging the ground. The most massive feature of
the whole structure, however, was the great chimney which housed in
its ample bosom from one to four fireplaces on the first floor, and sometimes another in the cellar. On later examples there may have been
fireplaces on the upper floors.

Often eight to twelve feet square, these chimneys supported the
main horizontal timbers and gave the whole house a rigidity it could
not otherwise have had. One of the fireplaces was much larger than
the others and incorporated a baking oven. Up to 1750 or thereabouts
these ovens were in the back of the fireplace. Later they were built to
one side of it. This fireplace served the kitchen, which also constituted
what we would call today the living room and dining room. In the
smallest houses this may have been the only room on the ground floor.
The general idea, though, seems to have been to start with either one

or two rooms and add more as they were needed or as conditions allowed.

This type of Early American house may have a room on each of the two opposite sides of the chimney, and from one to three rooms at the back along the third side of the stack. Very often the front side of the chimney, which formed a small space between the two front rooms, was used for the stairs to the upper floor, perhaps with the cellar stairs below them. In such a case the front door of the house would open into this tiny hall, which was called a porch or entry.

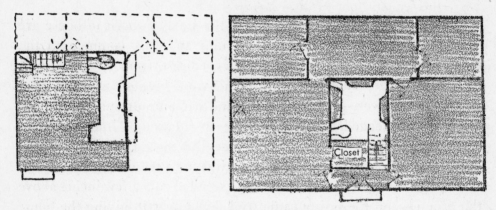

Floor plan showing how a single-room Early American grew into a central-chimney house.

There are other instances where a house with a single first-floor room has the front door opening into that room in the corner farthest from the chimney. The stairs may then be in the opposite corner, against the rear wall. Adding a second room at the other side of the chimney would leave the "porch" space as part of the first room. Such a house could be further extended by adding a lean-to at the rear, the full length of the house. After that, any additional space would be secured by turning the lean-to into a full two-story addition, or by adding an ell, or a straight extension to the first floor.

Quite a number of cottages were begun as a single-room plan, with the large chimney occupying one wall. The builder doubtless had visions of adding more rooms around the chimney at some future date.

But the fates were not kind, and they remain today as they were when they were so hopefully raised a couple of centuries ago.

Not a few of these houses started life as a single-story structure, often with a large attic space which could later be turned into useful rooms. If the main walls extended higher than the ceiling of the first floor, it would be called a one-and-a-half-story house, and the upstairs ceilings would slope at the sides where the roof came down. Other houses had two full stories and, more rarely, two and a half.

Instead of adding an extra full floor, it was common practice to increase the second-floor or attic headroom by using a gambrel roof in place of the ordinary pitched roof. A great many fantastic theories are quoted as facts regarding the gambrel roof. We shall go into the subject more thoroughly later, but it may be as well to state right here that the gambrel roof is neither a Dutch innovation nor an American invention. Such roofs were far from unknown in England and Europe in the sixteenth century. The use of such a roof on an Early American house therefore has little significance beyond the fact that it was the most suitable type for the existing conditions, or that the house owner wanted a roof of that kind.

In the case of the one-and-a-half-story house all the upstairs windows would be in the gables. In the others, the windows would probably correspond with those of the first floor, though often they were somewhat smaller, at least in height. All of these windows will be of the sash or "guillotine" type, with the upper half either fixed or movable only an inch or two, and the lower section capable of being raised a little short of its full height.

Shutters or blinds were not commonly used on these houses before the end of the eighteenth century. The first blinds had fixed louvers, and the rails and stiles were very narrow. Solid outside shutters were generally of paneled construction, sometimes with a peephole and sometimes without. These were more used in the Middle Atlantic states than elsewhere. The whole blind and shutter situation is, as a matter of fact, so confused that little reliance can be placed on them as a guide to original style or the age of the house.

On these wooden houses the roofs were practically always shingled, but the sides may have been covered with clapboards, flush boarding, weatherboards, or shingles. In all cases, except where shingle siding is used the corners of the building were finished off with a narrow board (four to six inches wide) that gives the appearance of a corner post.

In some parts of the country, the Early American houses of the central-stack type had walls of stone. In parts of Long Island and Pennsylvania, for example, field stone was sometimes used, but in Pennsylvania's counties of Berks, Lebanon, and Lancaster you will find walls built of ledge stone (traprock). These slabs of stone were often of considerable size, suggesting that the cutting, hauling, and hoisting into position involved a great deal more muscular effort and perspiration than we could afford to invest in such work today.

In New Jersey masons often used the red sandstone dumped by long-gone glaciers in its fields, and the Dutch, putting up their solid domiciles in both New Jersey and New York, showed a distinct partiality for a combination of stone walls and wooden gables.

Turning now to the interior, the early seventeen hundreds found it common practice to use white plaster for all or part of the walls. Sometimes we find horizontal boards forming a low wainscot or dado, and, generally in later houses, no wood on the walls except baseboards (mopboards or skirtings), and perhaps paneled areas below the windows. In other instances a compromise is effected by protecting the plaster with a chair rail, for in those days chairs were built more for utility than comfort, and ease could only be achieved by tilting them back against the wall.

More pretentious domiciles boasted of paneled walls or wainscots, and paneling or vertical boarding persisted over the fireplace for many long years. Today we often find such paneling either buried beneath multiple layers of wallpaper or coats of paint. We generally discover, too, that some soulless wight has ruined the largest panel by hacking a large hole through the middle of it to accommodate a stovepipe.

Floor boards of pine or oak ten to twenty inches wide are common, often an inch or more thick, with the joints halved. The corner posts and ceiling beams were left exposed during this period. Contrary to popular belief, these exposed beams were not left rough with the ax marks showing, nor were they boxed in. They were carefully worked over to obtain a smooth finish. In the earlier houses the undersides of the floor boards were exposed between the beams; in later years lath and plaster hid them. By 1727 mantel shelves began to make their

Typical low wainscoting. Detail shows capping and beaded-lap joint.

appearance, and within the next fifty years mantels, in other rooms than the kitchen, had become highly decorative features that gave small fireplaces the prominence they deserved.

Briefly, then, the salient features of the eighteenth-century New England type of Early American house are: a central chimney, a plain exterior having the eaves flush with the gables, simple window and door trim, low underpinning, plain, narrow corner boards, simple sheathed, plank, or paneled doors, sometimes with a plain, square row of lights over the front door. The roof would usually be a plain ridge type. Less often it would be a gambrel. These are the characteristic forms, but, as we must emphasize, there are many local and individual variations. For example, we have seen a number of roofs that are of the pitched type in front and gambrel in the rear, and others the reverse. We have come across dormers in very early gambrels and even in the pitched roofs. In such instances it has been quite impossible to determine whether or not these were later additions without tearing the walls apart, a procedure that the owners naturally contemplated with little enthusiasm.

## The Southern Early American

In the warmer climate of the South, the Early American house was somewhat like the Georgian in outward appearance, but was as severely simple as its northern counterpart. The fireplaces were built into the

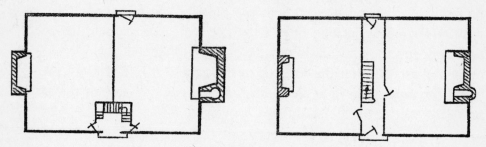

Floor plans of typical southern Early American houses.

end gables of the house, and there were often two stacks instead of one. In some houses the chimneys were inside the gable walls; in others they would project outside, beyond the wall line. It is often suggested that these external chimneys were an exclusive feature of warmer climates where the heat lost was of little consequence. Whether this is true or not, that fact did not deter owners from occasionally using external chimneys on Early American houses built in the chilly North.

The front door was located in the center of the front wall and opened into a hall or passage which gave access to the ground-floor rooms and provided space for the stairs. This hall or passage did not always extend straight through from the front of the house to the back,

in fact the rear part of it often formed a scullery whose principal ornament was a sink. Where there was no hall, the front door opened
directly into one of the rooms, the back door usually opening out of the
other room. The stairs would then be against the dividing wall.

These small houses were only one room deep, and the fireplaces occupied the middle of the gable walls. One was usually much larger
than the other to serve as a kitchen fireplace, and both chimneys infrequently incorporated fireplaces on the second floor also.

Externally, these houses, whether of wood, brick, or stone, were extremely plain. Window and door trim were mere flat strips of wood.
Some of the houses had their eaves extending slightly beyond the
gables, but for the most part they were flush.

Shingles were the commonest roof covering, but tiles and slates (or
thin stone) have been recorded on one or two brick or stone houses.
Not much attention was paid to the balance of the façade. Houses
with two windows at one side of the door and one at the other were
common, and the door in this case would be off center.

As far as the interiors are concerned, these houses follow pretty
much the same pattern as the central-stack type of house of the same
period.

## The Georgian House

All houses of the Georgian style have end chimneys just as the southern Early American houses do, but they show many variations that the
Early Americans do not. In all instances the proportions of the chimneys seem more carefully planned as an architectural feature. The
Georgian differed from the southern Early American in that they
were always two rooms deep. This provided an interior wall parallel
with the roof ridge. Quite frequently the chimneys were not built into
the gables, but were located some distance in from the end walls. In
such cases the fireplaces are not in the end walls, but in the center of
this cross wall separating the front room from the room behind it.
Sometimes the chimneys were in front of the roof ridge and sometimes

behind it, depending on the location of the cross walls with reference to the ridge.

Hipped roofs grew increasingly popular as time went on, so that the chimneys, standing clear, were much taller and more prominent. This chimney arrangement was, of course, indicative of the layout of the rooms whose fireplaces they served. The principal feature of the first-floor plan was the central hall extending from the front door to the back one. This hall was fairly wide, and the open stairs led up from it. On either side of the central hall were the principal rooms, usually four altogether. The foundation, as a rule, was set higher than in the case of the Early American, and the extra height helped give the

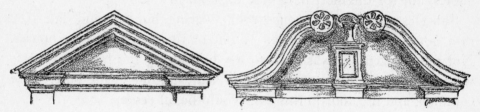

Early scroll and triangular pediments.

house a more imposing appearance, which was what everyone wanted.

Externally, the small Georgian house had a much less rugged appearance than the earlier style, but the biggest difference lay in the decorative features that architects call classic embellishments. While clapboards were used on the wooden houses they were generally beaded along their lower edge, or otherwise given a more dressy finish. Often the more formal clapboards were confined to the front of the house, and shingles used on the rear and side walls. But it was the windows and doorways that really were glorified.

Beautifully proportioned paneled doors were used, flanked by ornate pilasters supporting a pediment of the triangular, scrolled, or segmental kind. Several stone steps led up to the front door.

The windows, too, were set off by architraves, pediments, and the delicate moldings to which wood so readily lends itself. The corner boards gave way to simulated pilasters, dressed up with moldings, or to imitation quoins, and the overhanging eaves were supported by fancy cornices. Sometimes the eaves overhung the gables, and on other occasions were finished flush with a molded bargeboard. On hipped roofs, of course, the cornice was carried right around the ends. If the roof was of the gambrel type there would almost invariably be two or more dormers.

Somewhere around 1750 a form of window was used called the Palladian window, after the Italian architect, Andrea Palladio, who had introduced it two hundred years before. This was really a group

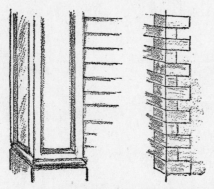

A simulated pilaster, and imitation
quoins.

of three windows, the central one being higher than those on each side and having a rounded top. This window was placed above the front door or porch and gave the upper part of the front wall just as imposing an appearance as the door and its surround did to the lower portion. Some of the carpenter-architects became so entranced by the Palladian window that they even put them in the gables at the attic-floor level. They also let their imagination run riot and conceived some weird combinations of shapes and sizes between the three window sections. Late in the century they sometimes added blinds to increase the size and importance of this decorative feature. In one case that we know of, the designer of a story-and-a-half Georgian, not to be out-done, installed a front door with full-length sidelights and rounded door top that looked for all the world like an oversize Palladian window.

Georgian interiors grew to be extremely elaborate even in the smaller houses. During the early part of the period the ceiling beams were left exposed, though the spaces between them were plastered. In the later years buried beams and ceilings plastered all over became the

Palladian windows such as this were an important feature of a Georgian house.

vogue. In these houses you will likewise find differences in the wall treatment. Generally speaking, they followed the same trends as the Early Americans, but they went a great deal further. In the beginning the walls were plastered halfway down, the lower part consisting of a simple wainscot of horizontal boards. After 1750 or so these walls, too, were plastered all the way down to the mopboard.

Interior doors were of the paneled variety, often with applied moldings in place of the solid integral ones of the earlier types. There may be paneling over the wooden mantel. The wide oak or pine floors of the previous period were still used, though in later days more trouble seems to have been taken to match them in width, and they were, on the whole, somewhat narrower.

Throughout this period the tendency was gradually to remove from sight all structural features such as corner posts and beams. The interiors, like the exteriors, began to be designed as units, with the proportions and shapes and decorations, such as plaster cornices, more carefully studied. Fireplace openings were made smaller, and those who could afford such luxuries decorated the fireplaces with Dutch tiles. Oftener they had to be content with marble slabs.

All of the internal features and most of the external ones catalogued thus far apply both to the wooden Georgians and the brick and stone ones. In the late examples of the small brick Georgian, we sometimes run across one that was covered with stucco. On rare examples we may also find that the original wooden façade was hidden behind a single layer of beautiful pink brick. One practically general feature of the brick and stone structures is the use of wood for all window and door casings and trims. Bare brick around openings was unusual.

## *Greek Revival Houses*

From the Atlantic to far beyond the Mississippi the countryside abounds with these classic temples of the Greek Revival era. From the turn of the nineteenth century on they gained in favor. Spreading to the expanding West, they reached the height of popularity there about 1850. With their white columns, pretentious porches, and obviously Grecian motifs they are not hard to identify. Frequently one end of the house will face the road; in other words the end becomes the front and contains the "front" door.

The Greek Revival house always has deep overhanging eaves, especially at the gable ends on pitched roofs. One of its most noticeable features is the heavy cornice running either completely across the gable or returned part way across the end of the house. Dentils, those toothlike projections, were applied to cornices on both houses and porches with lavish abandon.

It is interesting also to observe the great variety of gable windows on the third or attic floor of these houses. While they are often rectangular, there are many other forms such as quarter- or half-circle, diamond, triangular, etc. Dormer windows were never used on houses of this period.

The inside porch of the early houses was pushed outside by the introduction of the central-hall floor plan, outgrowing its modesty displayed in the Georgian period by becoming the principal decorative feature of the façade of the Greek Revival house. The fronts of these houses derived their interest from the use of Greek or Roman porch columns surmounted by an imposing roof, and in the corner pilasters. The doorways were often slightly recessed.

Greek Revival windows are always generous in proportion and widely spaced. In the more elaborate houses there is an architrave over each window. At the end of the eighteenth century and the beginning of the nineteenth the Palladian window was adapted to the Greek Revival style by chopping off the head of the center section and making the three parts all the same height. On the first floor, windows were lengthened so that they reached the floor. Some of these had three sashes, and when two of them were raised a person of normal height could walk through. A little later casements replaced the tall sashes, forming what are known as french windows.

Up till the nineteenth century all these windows were mounted in elaborate frames. Afterwards the frames were simplified, and those in brick walls, formerly flush with the face, were set back in the wall, exposing the surrounding brickwork. At this time some of the houses were built with much flatter roofs, and although chimneys were likely to pop out almost anywhere they were not so noticeable.

Except for the impressive porches, the small Greek Revival houses were much less ornate than the Georgian, but more severely classical, both inside and out.

[ 48 ]

## Hallmarks of Houses

These, then, are the main features of the three principal styles of houses you may encounter in your search for one that you would like to call your own. But the chances are that you may not at once discern the telltale features beneath the "improvements" and additions of more recent years. Many a contradictory clue may be uncovered, but let that not disturb you. In these smaller houses it matters little where architectural purity begins or ends. If the house has charm and appeal and fulfills your needs, that is the house for you. Forget the pedigree and be content with the resolve to preserve what is good, and adapt the rest with conscience and with care.

# CHAPTER III

# How Old Is My House?

IT IS only natural that an owner of an old-time house should want to know when it was built. There is a fascination in picturing the mode of life of the successive generations that have lived in it; of recalling to mind the historic times through which the house has existed; and the changes that have taken place in its surroundings as the tide of civilization has risen about it. And age, of course, is an important factor in authentic restoration. But in the absence of documentary evidence there can be few more difficult tasks than that of attempting to estimate the year, let alone the decade, in which the house was reared. Too often it is exasperating even trying to decide where to begin. The house as it stands today may, like the Irishman's knife, have little left of the original structure, and changes may have been made that it is hopeless to try and trace.

No house can be lived in for one hundred and fifty or two hundred years without undergoing innumerable changes. Families grow and need more space; things wear out and need replacing; and now and again the local carpenter must be called in to make "modern" additions and improvements both inside and out.

Even architectural style is often of little help. It is rare indeed to find a small house so pure in architecture that it will readily fall into one of the major classifications—Early American, Georgian, or Greek Revival—in every detail. Characteristic features of any one of these may have been submerged by those of other styles, or of no style at all. Then, too, it occurs rather often that only one unit of a house is original, and even that may be disguised so well as to make identification difficult. In the old days fires were quite common, thanks to faulty chimneys, so that the rebuilding of a portion of many an old house was necessary at some time or other.

Local building customs, the kinds of materials used, and the geographical location all enter into the picture, not to mention the individual whims of the carpenter-builder whose creations have been known to puzzle even an expert. It will be only by summing up all the characteristics of your house that you can obtain a clue as to its age. Usually if you come within twenty-five years of being correct you will be doing very well!

The most dependable source of information is documentary evidence, such as the original deed, an old will, or receipts with the dates for materials used in building the house. But even these cannot be relied upon unless they include a detailed description of the house. That is why even old maps are not acceptable evidence. A map may show a house where yours now stands, but there is nothing to prove that it is the same house. The original house may have been burned, or even blown away in a hurricane! A title search, especially in country districts, often fails to reveal the desired information for the reason that deeds were not recorded in the early days, or, if they were, they were inaccurately kept. And sometimes early records were lost or destroyed by fire. Finally, it is generally best to discount the recollections of local wiseacres, and all memory and hearsay, especially that passed on through several generations. It is rarely trustworthy.

To turn to the other side of the picture, however, luck may be in your favor. Some houses have their dates built in. In brick houses, particularly, the date of construction may be worked into a gable or a chimney. Occasionally anchor irons were made in the form of figures to indicate the date. And we have seen several instances in which the date was cut into the stone wall of a cellar or in the timbers of a central-chimney foundation. But the average old-time builder did not make things so simple for us.

Failing any direct evidence, an approximation of age can best be arrived at through the investigation of a variety of features and striking a balance. These details include the framing, brick- or stonework, foundations, windows, hardware, woodwork, fireplaces, and so on. The part played by architectural style has already been discussed. It must, however, be remembered that the location of the house may have considerable influence on the date of these features and the year of their adoption in any particular instance. Since most of the customs, fashions, and methods originated in the East, the date of their introduction there should be a more or less reliable guide to the date of their adoption farther west. For example, a type of window or glass used in 1750 on the eastern coast may not have reached settlements beyond the Mississippi till ten years later. In the majority of instances, then, these approximations will be broad and constitute no more than intelligent guesses. They should be treated as such.

One of the simplest of clues lies in the use of hand-wrought nails. If you find them in the woodwork you may be fairly sure that your house was built before 1795. If they are in the floor boards the house may be even older, because floors were sometimes replaced when they had become worn or cracked. If you find them holding down the bottom edges of clapboards the house is probably even older still.

Generally speaking, the older the house, the closer it hugs the ground, except in the Cape Cod style, which even today is built practically at ground level. The underpinning of all types of houses was usually of local stone, except in the South, where brick underpinning was often used for the very early brick houses. This is not surprising, since bricks were made in Jamestown in 1611! In other sections brick foundations occasionally appeared after 1730, but underpinning of stone continued to be the most popular, even for brick houses in the northern colonies, at least till 1750.

An interesting feature of the early stone foundations is that they were laid dry, i.e., without anything to hold them together. Lime mortar was used in the northern colonies as early as 1700, but there were many districts in which the lime was not available. Very often the joints between the stones have been pointed up with mortar at a much later date, when efforts were made to keep the cellar dry and the house warm. Fortunately it is very easy to tell whether or not this was done—by pulling out a chunk of the mortar. It can then be seen whether or not the stones are actually laid in mortar.

In many of the houses built in the late seventeen hundreds cellars were very often built with rough stone on three sides, but the tops of the front walls were more carefully built of dressed stone. This applies especially to cases where some of the foundation showed.

Another prominent feature of the old houses that changed considerably with time was the windows. Unfortunately the windows were often the first things to be replaced and enlarged. The sash or guillotine window was introduced in the East in 1715. The stiles and bars were of very light construction, often being not more than an inch thick, and only slightly broader. On the other hand, the muntin bars that held the glass were very thick and the glass was set flush in them, giving the window its characteristic old-fashioned appearance. These broad muntins were used until 1780 or thereabouts.

The earliest houses had tiny panes of glass, but a great number of them. The panes were often no larger than $4 \times 6$ inches, and there may have been anywhere from eighteen to twenty-four to a window. As time went by, the size of the pane used grew larger. By 1775 even small houses had panes as large as $8 \times 10$ inches, and more pretentious residences had even bigger ones. Houses built a decade after the Revolution often had only twelve lights to a window, six in each sash. Before that time it was more usual to have a larger number in the upper sash, say twelve over eight or nine over six, but there is no definite rule about this. Often it seems that the size of the window had something to do with it. Where only the bottom part of a large window opened, it was an advantage to have it lighter and therefore easier to lift.

The most common dormer window built during the eighteenth century was the square-headed type, topped by a pediment or triangular gable, but after 1745 occasional examples of semicircular-headed ones appeared. After 1760 it was common practice to put lights in the upper panels of doors. But there were no sidelights around the doors till after the Revolution. The first of these sidelights had wooden muntins and square panes. The fancy metal ones came in later.

The famous Palladian windows were introduced shortly before 1750 and did not degenerate into flat-topped triple windows until about thirty years later. Similarly the Georgian doorways remained square-topped till 1756 or so, when semicircular arches were used to surmount them. Elliptical fanlights were not used until post-Revolutionary days. Other details that were not introduced until Revolution-

Three types of dormers. Georgian at the left, and an early New England gambrel type.

ary times were locks on doors and a baking oven alongside the fireplace. Previously these ovens had been located in the back wall of the huge open fireplaces. In their new position they achieved the dignity of a separate flue. Cellar fireplaces are not found in houses built before 1750, and then never were common. Mantelpieces, on the other hand, date back as far as 1725.

Somewhere during the last decade of the eighteenth century, when wallpapers were a luxury in large houses, the vogue of stenciling walls and floors in the smaller houses reached its peak. Sometimes even the risers of the stairs were decorated in this manner, and excellent examples of this are found in some northern Ohio houses. The painting of houses began around 1737, but it was not until 1800 that commercial paint was available and houses blossomed into color on a large scale.

# How Old Is My House?

Hardware, too, may throw a little light on dates, though most small houses lost their original latches and hinges long ago. But even when it seems that this is the case, it is as well to examine every door throughout the house carefully, attic and cellar and closet doors in particular, for an odd latch or hinge that has been overlooked. The early butterfly hinges were largely displaced by HL hinges after 1750, and cast-iron butt hinges made their appearance in 1775. Early latches had thumbpieces that were round, flat, and of very thin wrought iron. Those made after 1800 were thicker, bean-shaped, and scooped. The factory-made Norfolk latch, with its oblong plate and cast-iron handle, came into use shortly after 1800, but the cast-iron latch did not appear till 1840.

Although many Colonial houses are without them, shutters and blinds were customarily found in all parts of the country. The earliest type of blind, used till about 1760, had fixed slats. After that time the adjustable-slat type became the vogue, except in some areas, such as Dutchess County, New York, where solid shutters were used throughout the eighteenth century. In that state the slat blinds were not used till the nineteenth century. In some states the year 1800 witnessed the adoption of front-door blinds with fixed slats.

These, then, are some of the uncertain fingers that point to dates in housebuilding history. Doubtless numbers more will be gleaned from the following pages in which the origins and uses of various items and features are gone into at length. Nevertheless, the fact remains that the dating of houses is far from being an exact science and often calls for more detective skill than the solution of many an intricate whodunit plot!

# CHAPTER IV

# Preserving the Intangibles

WHEN you set out to buy an old house you generally have a fairly good idea of what you want. But it is pretty certain that in the end you will compromise a little here and there, perhaps sacrificing that extra bathroom for an overwhelming view, or accepting a Greek Revival cottage with a perfect room layout in place of that exquisite, but cramped, Early American on which you had set your heart. Life is like that.

In any event, the day will inevitably come when the house is seen, looked over, prodded here and there with a knife blade to be sure there are neither termites nor rot, cash planked down, papers signed, and the house is yours. It may be in livable condition, ready to move into, or it may need quite a few repairs or alterations first. In either case it is always wise to consider the house as a whole and not attempt any piecemeal changes. Even so little a thing as changing a kitchen sink or installing a new type of water heater may have repercussions you did not expect.

Any changes you make presumably will be for greater convenience and comfort, better appearance, or economy of operation. But since you have deliberately bought a very old house, you will, undoubtedly, want to preserve as much of its old-time air as possible. This means that you will have to think twice before you decide to move water or drain pipes, or cut holes in walls or floors, or do more modernizing than is absolutely essential. And it is astonishing how many of our preconceived ideas of convenience and comfort we can dump overboard without regret when they run afoul of sentiment, feeling, or taste. On the other hand, with careful consideration, based on knowledge, it is unbelievable how many opposing ideas can be reconciled and awkward compromises circumvented.

But when all of these things have been duly considered, nine times out of ten you will find that you do need to make a number of changes both inside and out. Unless someone else has already done the work, there will usually be alterations and additions to make, some of them possibly quite extensive. Old houses in their original or even late-nineteenth-century condition are notably lacking in what we consider the minimum essentials for modern living. Many of them suffer from one of three major defects—rooms that are too small, bathrooms and closets that are too few or entirely lacking. Some have windows that are badly placed or not big enough; they have tilted floors, ill-fitting doors, faulty chimneys, and dangerous stairs. Others need an augmented water supply, electricity (sometimes more of a luxury than a necessity), or a sewage-disposal system. Then, too, on the outside there will be the question of what to do with that accumulation of gingerbread that hides the fine lines of the old house—the fretwork decorations, "new style" doors and windows, hoods and decorative iron rails on the front steps, and so on. More serious are the additions, such as attached bays, pergolas, or porches and unsightly dormers which have involved changes to the original structure.

All of this work can be classified under one of two heads—restoration and remodeling. Restoration, usually but not always, is carried out for aesthetic reasons; remodeling for more practical ones. Restoration is simply rehabilitation—putting the building back into its original condition. It may involve anything from the replacement of a rotted beam to the removal of an octagonal bay, or the eradication of paint to reveal the mellowed surface of old pine. It may mean removal or replacement, but never addition.

Remodeling, on the other hand, may call for modifications, additions, or radical alterations to the original structure, and possibly the sacrifice of some of its distinguishing characteristics, so as to adapt it for modern living. It is a much more drastic procedure than restoration, and needs to be handled with even greater care. It means changes in shape, style, accommodations, or design. That is why it is an operation not to be undertaken lightly or ignorantly. Charm and a feeling of fitness are subtle things that can vanish at a touch. Retaining them is as difficult as creating them, and neither is a job for the amateur without intensive study.

*Complete* remodeling of an old-time house is not to be advocated, for two reasons. It is usually more expensive, and, in the end, less satisfactory than building anew, and the inevitable destruction or mutilation of an old building in the process is always regrettable if not downright vandalism!

The question of what should be done regarding appearance and architectural style is another matter that needs to be given considerable thought.

While it is very nice to have a house that represents some definite architectural style, it is not worth while spending much time, effort, and money to achieve that end. Very few small houses exist that are, or ever were, pure examples of any one style. Even if they began life as a comparatively pure type, they were probably modified or added to over the years, and the total result may be either generally good or generally bad. In any case it is usually pretty hopeless to try and restore to any old house all its original architectural features. For one thing we cannot always be sure how pure an example it was in the beginning; secondly because alterations may have to be so drastic that the air of antiquity is lost with them. Finally because, if we have an inoffensive house, each part of which is really old and represents a stage of gradual development, little is gained by stripping it down to its original bare essentials. Securing perfect harmony of design and line is a laudable aim, but it is not worth going overboard about and running the risk of spoiling charm and interest. Dissonance has its uses in architecture as well as in music.

Lots of the earlier houses began to grow almost as soon as they were built. We recall one particularly nice Early American, central-stack-type house that was built in two halves. The first portion, erected in

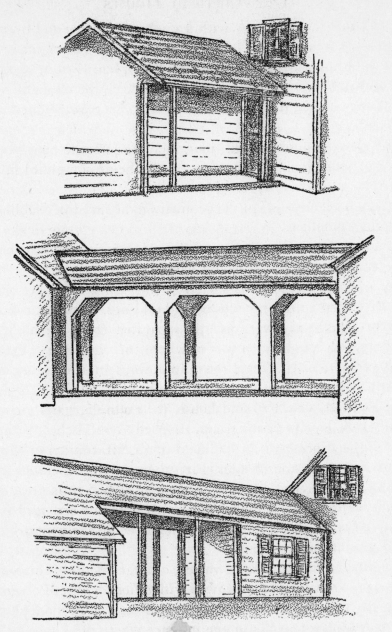

Three methods of tying together outbuildings—a recessed porch
and two types of breezeway.

1765, consisted of a chimney with a kitchen fireplace and oven, and a small fireplace at one side in an adjoining room. The chimney occupied most of one wall of the two-room floor plan. Fifteen years later a pair of rooms were added to the other side of the chimney, which now became a central stack. No more fireplaces were added, but a second front door was installed, the purpose of which is a mystery. Thereafter extensions and additions, including porches and bay windows, were made from time to time, the last being completed in about 1840.

This is a good example of the problems to be faced in deciding just how far we should go in restoration. It is also a sample of the variations in original layout that you will find are far commoner than the classic works on old houses would lead one to suspect.

In a great many old houses such as this, extra space for various activities was acquired by adding outbuildings. In the warmer climates these buildings were usually separated from the house, and often from one another. In places where the winters are long and severe it is more usual to find the outbuildings attached to the house, generally strung together like beads on a string.

Many an old New England house, for example, starts off with a modest ell composed of a storeroom attached to the kitchen. From that point on, the appendages grow like a dog's tail, limited only by the imagination of the householder. First there might be a woodshed, a covered passage to the backhouse, a hen house, barn, milk shed, stable, carpenter's shop, wagon shed, and springhouse, all arranged so that you can get from one to the other without facing the wintry blast or wading knee-deep in snow.

If your house has acquired a variety of attachments of this sort you may want to keep some and do away with others. Some, of course, can be converted to various uses, while others may be in too bad a condition, too odoriferous (as in one instance where the kitchen ell had been used for years as a turkey slaughterhouse!), or a fire hazard preventing proper access to the rest of the buildings. In many instances what appears to be an unsightly collection of sheds and shacks can be given some architectural form and unity at little expense. All that is needed is some unifying element, such as the extension of a roof or gutter line, or the installation of similar types of windows, siding, or trim. Often, all that is required is a coat of paint all around.

Where the buildings are separated by uncomfortable gaps, they can often be tied together by breezeways or loggias or recessed porches, providing the style of these structures does not clash with the character of the house.

All of these points should be carefully studied before calling in the wreckers and abolishing what might have turned out to be a cozy, quiet, and remote study for the master of the house.

In both restoring and remodeling it is highly important that we do nothing to vitiate the old-time atmosphere or debase the character of the house and its external appendages. To this end it is necessary to observe certain rules, the most important of which is never to mix the old with the new so that the difference is obvious. This statement conjures up recollections of a certain kitchen fireplace that collapsed when work was being done on the chimney. In rebuilding it the old brick and stones were replaced in the fireback, but the mason, dissatisfied with the shabby used brick, on his own initiative carefully restored the facing with brand-new bricks. The total result was a fireplace that spoiled the feeling of the whole room. Needless to say, it pleased no one, least of all the owner, who effected a temporary improvement by painting all the bricks dead black until they could be replaced.

Such catastrophes can be avoided by seeing that restorations are effected with old materials, or at least with materials that look as authentic as the original. It also helps to keep a close watch on the workmen. One enthusiastic carpenter who came for a brief instant into our lives demonstrated this need in no uncertain manner. Restoring the staircase to its original form alongside the chimney, he came across a strange bulge in the brickwork that broke the line of the stringer. Heedless of our admonition to fit the stair to the house and not the house to the stair, he proceeded to hack away on the offending bricks. Before this sacrilege was discovered he had gouged a huge hole in the back of our beloved bake oven. He never knew how close he come to sudden violent extinction.

The second point is to match carefully details such as moldings, methods of making joints and finishing surfaces. Most of these are readily dated and differ to a noticeable degree from modern substitutes. There are, for example, certain moldings used for mantels in the eighteenth century that have not been commercially duplicated since. Likewise some early door-panel moldings were made in one piece with the stiles. On modern doors the moldings are applied separately, and the difference is immediately obvious, particularly if an old door is duplicated by a modern one close by. To retain the old-time atmosphere it is necessary to stick to old methods and designs. It is surprising how many people can tell one from the other, and no one likes to advertise his ignorance even to friends.

In remodeling, the same principles apply equally as regards materials, style, and method of construction, with the one exception that it will be a practical impossibility to employ braced-frame construction on additional buildings today. A study of the following chapters will give a very good idea of what these things usually consisted in the various periods between 1700 and 1850.

External alterations or replacements to roofs, walls, windows, or chimneys have to be carefully watched. Yesterday's chimney on a 200-year-old house is not only incongruous but unsightly. Proportions too are important. Changes in the height of the underpinning, apparent or real, may not only alter the balance of the house but make it look as though it is gingerly sitting on the ground instead of rising out of it. Lowering flower beds to expose cellar windows as a "cure" for dampness, removing the bottom course of siding, or raising the house to deepen the cellar, will all have this effect. Pointing an old foundation with new cement will sometimes do the same thing unless its color is toned down to blend with the old mortar. These examples are probably sufficient to show the principles involved. The most important thing, however, is to do nothing in a hurry.

## Preserving the Intangibles

In some few instances it is essential to make changes before moving into the house, but more often it is possible to postpone alterations until later. It is probably trite to say that it is always wiser to live in a house over a period of time before attempting to make any important changes. Haste not only makes waste in the undoing of mistakes, but breeds disappointment and dissatisfaction. Ideas change as the new surroundings become familiar, and experience with the layout is a useful guide in making and carrying out plans.

### Planning Alterations

In planning changes to your house it is a good idea to list them under the head of restoration or remodeling. Separating the jobs in this way helps you to judge which are most urgent and important and which can wait till convenience (or, perhaps, finances) allows. Remodeling will probably have to come first, as practical considerations always must take the precedence over aesthetic ones, at least for most of us. And the first step should be to put down every projected change or addition on paper.

Whether or not finances are going to determine what alterations you can carry out, the whole project should be thoroughly thought out in the beginning. This is the wise thing to do even if only a portion of the scheme can be put into effect immediately. Some practical souls work out a three-year plan or a five-year plan for their houses, but most of us go ahead with no plan at all. We just dive right in, tearing things apart, or adding this or that because it seems a good idea at the moment. An otherwise intelligent friend of ours, using this piecemeal method, changed his closets and bookshelves four times in five years, much to the disgust of the carpenter who was forced to wreck his own good work. Proper planning in the beginning is much easier on the pocketbook and on the house.

One of the first things to be decided is the use to which the house is going to be put. Do you intend to use it for summer vacations, for winter week ends also, or is there a chance in the not-too-distant future that it will become your permanent, year-round home? You can save yourself considerable expense, and often extensive alterations later on, if you decide these points beforehand.

A second point to be settled is whether or not you wish to restore the house to its original state, in keeping with the period in which it was built, or whether you merely want to remodel it for comfortable living. In either case will it be adequate to the needs and size of your family?

The purpose to which you are going to put your house will influence tremendously the amount and kind of materials going into these alterations. For instance, if you are not going to use it in cold weather, a simple heating apparatus will serve for the chilly nights which we get occasionally during the summer in many parts of the country. For winter use, on the other hand, you will not only need an adequate heating system, but some insulation. Wall insulation is almost sure to be necessary on a wooden house, as you will realize when you discover fine snow drifting through the paneling, as we have done. Such walls are far from windproof, and many a handsome clapboard hides a leak. Summer is the time to make certain that fuel can be delivered to your door when the snow is on the ground. This has been known to involve the choice between laying a long and expensive driveway or a winter in Florida or California—a matter that can be embarrassing if it is overlooked.

Another point to consider is whether or not your family is likely to increase or decrease over the years. Will the children be going away to camp or school? And do not forget that a house that is used as a summer home might require several more bedrooms than would a year-round house where you will be likely to have fewer visitors at any one time.

There can, of course, be no argument that a modern kitchen and a modern bathroom are essentials. For year-round occupancy, most families would demand two baths. Even if the house is in the dead of the country, none of us wants to spend his time turning the Sunday

Pine is more effective in an old-type kitchen than enameled
steel.

Adapting a modern sink to an old-fashioned kitchen.

roast on a spit over the open fire, or tramping to the reading room at the bottom of the garden path.

Modern kitchens and bathrooms do not, of course, have to be all chromium, white-enameled steel, or tile and glass. Hospital-type fixtures have no place in the Colonial house, nor are they necessary.

Modern bathroom fixtures are much better disguised in any house.

Wood was the most commonly used material in the early days, and a great many admirable and lovely things can be done with it. Old pine cabinets, cupboards, closets, tables, and work surfaces can give a kitchen that old-time look without detracting from its efficiency or sanitary standards. Linoleum tops and floors provide washable surfaces, and a hard-surfaced paint can be used to liven up the appearance if used with discrimination.

In bathrooms the woodwork can profitably be used to provide flat surfaces around the washbowl, with cabinets beneath, instead of the unsightly, antiquated, plated legs. Toilets, which have not been improved in appearance since their naked torsos were exposed at the turn of the century, are much better enclosed in a flat-topped cabinet with a square hinged seat and cover. Woods, with a natural finish or painted, will, in this way, give a trim and smart finish that is more up to date than any of the so-called modern groups of unrelated bathroom units.

Accommodations can be increased in a number of ways besides converting the woodshed into a one-room apartment complete with bath. If the house has a gable roof and sufficiently strong timbers,

One solution of the closet problem, using
attic space.

there may be room under the ridge if you can find a way of providing light and air. Large gable windows or dormers may be added. If dormers are not permissible, architecturally speaking, on your particular style of house, maybe they can be used on the rear slope of the roof. But see that they are in proportion—neither skimpy nor overlarge. The long, continuous dormer is always ugly and will spoil the lines of any roof. Avoid it like the plague!

No old house has sufficient closets. The sloping top-floor ceiling of any one-and-a-half- or two-and-a-half-story house provides a golden opportunity for doing something about this. Without too much sacrifice of space, here is a place to build closets. A section of cupboards or chests containing drawers may be built up from the floor as high as the bend in the ceiling will permit. If there are eyebrow windows, these closets or cabinets may be built around them so as not to shut off the light. Another means of adding closet room is to put up a ceiling-height partition about four feet from the wall. Add a simple closet door, and shelves and a hanger rail inside, and there you are. If there should happen to be a window in the section you partition off, so much the better. A window in a closet is an excellent arrangement, unless it robs a room of needed light and ventilation.

Other closets may be built under staircases. Very often one of the small bedrooms of an old house is converted into a bathroom. Sometimes a portion of this room can be made into a closet, too. Occasionally small closets can be tucked in at the end of a hall, at the sides of chimney breasts, or over and around fireplaces.

Locating the bathroom or bathrooms is a matter that calls for considerable thought. Usually one of the small bedrooms has to be sacrificed for this purpose, unless there is a convenient landing with space to spare. If possible a room over the kitchen should be used for the sake of economy. The water-supply and drain pipes will be that much shorter. Sometimes a second bathroom, or a half-bathroom (lavatory and toilet) can be placed in an adjoining room, with the fixtures against the same wall, and thus use the same drainpipe and vent.

It is a great convenience, especially where there are young children in the family, to have a half-bathroom on the first floor. This might be placed under the stair, at the end of the hall, or partitioned off from a too large pantry.

When you come to consider the installation of a heating system you have to remember that walls in old houses are always thin and rarely are capable of offering sanctuary to pipes and ducts. The possibility of having to put up false walls or casings has therefore to be taken into account. Another thing to remember is that the unaccustomed heat will inevitably cause all the woodwork to shrink. This can be offset to some extent by the use of a humidifier to keep the air from getting dry.

[ 68 ]

## Preserving the Intangibles

If it should be necessary to knock out a wall in order to make a room bigger or rearrange partitions, be sure to survey the whole situation thoroughly first. If it is a stud wall, see that there are no pipes or electrical conduits running through it that it will be difficult to locate elsewhere. And be sure it does not incorporate a post that will have to be replaced with a beam to support the floor or wall above it. Check the ceiling heights and floor levels to be sure there will be no difficulty in hiding the gap between them. In many instances the studs rest on walls or joists. If the partition is of the board-and-plaster type, there will be a pair of joists or beams with a space between them to hold the board. And in practically all instances there will be a gap in the flooring that will have to be filled, a situation that is not improved by the floor boards of one room running at right angles to those of the other room.

If the two rooms you are throwing into one are of different characters, you may have considerable trouble in matching them. One wall may be all plaster, while the other has a dado. Likewise the ceiling in one room may have exposed beams going in a direction opposite to those in the other room, or it may have none at all. So note all these features well before you begin to tear things down.

# CHAPTER V

# Trifles That Make Perfection

THE ideal old house would be an unspoiled one. It would have all of its original features intact, and no later additions that were out of keeping with its period and style. Each detail of material and workmanship and each fixture and fitting, such as hinges and latches, would be authentic in workmanship and design. Unfortunately such unspoiled old houses are far rarer than the poet's day in June, and it goes without saying that any old-time house you buy today will require considerable fixing to make it as it was in that far-off day when the builder finally gathered up his tools and turned it over to its first proud owner. Most of them, in fact, will need considerable restoring.

The prime purpose of restoration is to eliminate later additions and changes, both inside and outside of the house. If this is properly done, the old-time atmosphere and quaint charm of the house will be preserved, together with that homelike quality of peaceful domesticity which, for want of a better term, we call that lived-in feeling. Of course, even in old houses, it is possible to have too much of a good thing! No one wants to live in a museum or to turn his home into an antiquated stage setting as a background for even the most gracious and leisurely living. Perfection can be as abhorrent in a house as in a person, and in our enthusiasm for recapturing the old-time spirit we must not go to extremes. In other words, we do have to take into consideration the possibility that some features which our house has acquired over the years may be desirable from the standpoint of present-day living. The guiding principle here is whether or not they are in harmony with the rest of the house.

(*a*)  One man would tear off this sagging ell.

(*b*)  Another would see its architectural possibilities and
acquire a useful extension.

(*c*)  But it could also be widened and remodeled to give
emergency sleeping space.

[ 71 ]

# Old American Houses

Most of us realize that we can successfully furnish an old house with articles of varying ages and styles, provided we use discrimination. Because we have a house built in 1720 we do not have to furnish it throughout with things made in that year. That is not the way it was done in these small houses. Our forefathers accumulated odd pieces over the years, and, since we are not living in 1720 ourselves, we also may be excused for exhibiting that natural tendency. The same thing applies in connection with some of the features of the house itself. Although not original, such features may be useful and, being inoffensive, are better retained. Such later additions, if they are in keeping, sometimes add a graceful note and serve to remind us that houses are not static things, but grow and evolve along with the people who live in them. Even so, common sense and a knowledge of the fundamentals are needed to help us decide what is best retained and what should be thrown through the window.

We have to consider well the various features of the house that caused it to appeal to us in the beginning. These are the features to be preserved so long as they are in good taste. It is a good idea to study other old houses, or pictures of representative examples, and study books on the subject (no one book can cover all phases), and try to discover how the early builder worked out his problems. Oftentimes helpful ideas may be gleaned from other houses in the neighborhood, for details frequently are localisms not found elsewhere. Then, too, the builder of your house might well have put up a number of houses near by, basically the same as yours, but differing, perhaps, in size and other minor respects. But never forget that a house which is a mixture of ill-assorted detail and unmatched styles or materials can please no one with a sense of the fitness of things.

The keynote in restoration should be harmony, whether applied to the relation of the house to the outbuildings, to roof lines, to the size and balance of the house chimney (if rebuilding is necessary), to external embellishments of any kind, to fenestration, doors, and trim —or, in fact, anything that goes to make a good style.

In approaching the job of restoration, an ugly, oversized porch very often heads the list of things to be removed. On the other hand, in its proper place a porch can be a joy to those who love fresh air and the outdoors, with due protection from insect pests and the weather. On an Old Colonial house the place for such a porch is off

Removing the porch and restoring the chimney brings an old Colonial back to life.

to one side, in the angle between the house and the ell, or in the rear. Careful attention to the roof line and the proportions of your porch will go a long way toward keeping this addition as unobtrusive as it should be. What all of this means is that any porch which disfigures the front or ends of the house should be ripped off without a second thought. Porches which hide themselves from the public gaze may be reprieved if they can be modified to match the general architectural style of the house.

— Octagonal bay windows have no place in Colonial houses, and square ones or the rounded bow windows need to be used on Georgian-style houses with restraint. The effect of a square bay can sometimes be obtained by recessing a window sufficiently to provide a window bottom no more than a foot deep. In brick walls this breaks the wall line very little. A shallow bow window is better because it makes no sharp break at all. There are other means of letting in more light and expanding the view, such as the so-called picture window. Such a window, however, should keep to the pane sizes of the other windows, and it should be confined to the back of the house, if possible. Such things are permissible if carefully designed, but of course they are not authentic, and it is much better to do without them if you can. In any case, if your house is afflicted with a big, Victorian bay sticking out like a bad case of mumps, take it off!

Technically, dormer windows are permissible only in Georgian-style houses; actually, you will find them on practically all kinds except the pure Greek Revival. They are rare but not unknown on the central-chimney Early Americans, and many a gambrel roof sports anywhere from two to six. Since so many of these were used on small houses, either as original features or very early additions, we can have little quarrel with them. The only requirement is that they do not spoil the appearance of the house. This, of course, they can very easily do if they are not of the right size or type. Removal of dormers is a major operation, and unless some satisfactory substitute can be found, it is much better to compromise by remodeling them to eliminate their objectionable features.

It goes without saying that gingerbread trim should come off immediately. When once you have determined the basic style of your house, you should be able to tell what is original and what is later decoration.

Before beginning to rip down the various appendages tagged onto the rear of the house, examine them carefully. In more than one instance the summer kitchen or woodshed has been discovered to be as old, or older than, the house and to have quite a little architectural merit. In such a case it is often better to rehabilitate it, or even move it to a more convenient or useful spot, than to destroy it. If you look

at your house from all angles you will very likely find that an outbuilding or two lends interest by breaking the monotony of the line
and form.

A good way to check the age of the outbuilding against that of the
house is to compare the details of their framing. In the old days even
sheds were built on the same lines as the houses, with hewn beams
pegged together. Often the sill of a shed or other outbuilding would
consist of a huge timber, over which it was necessary to step when
entering the doorway. On good structures the upright posts would be
tenoned into this.

Generally speaking, it is bad policy to destroy outbuildings, because
they usually provide a simple and inexpensive means of extending the
house and at the same time retaining the old-time structural features
that are common to both. It is both difficult and expensive to try to
duplicate these old buildings today, and what you get will not have
that old-fashioned air that distinguishes these early structures, however humble they may be.

You will, naturally, want to restore all the old fireplaces that you
find in your house. If they are bricked or boarded up, it is a simple
matter to open them. But no fireplace should be used, even to burn
rubbish, till every flue has been examined and tested. Many an old-
time house has not survived this initial experiment, for reasons which
are discussed at length later on. Each fireplace should be examined
closely to see whether or not it has been reduced in size since it was
first built. At the same time a hunt may be organized for old paneling
and cupboards above the fireplace, features often hidden under paint,
paper, or even plaster!

Baking ovens, too, should be unblocked and, where necessary, re-
paired or even rebuilt. Many a one of these has been whittled down
to make room for a new stair or closet, or bobbed where it extended
through an outside wall. These are some of the most interesting features of the old-time houses which the moderns of the nineties took
great delight in hiding or mutilating. Restoring them is always a
particular pleasure.

# Old American Houses

One thing that you will rarely find surviving in a very old house is the original front door. If the door itself is there, it may have been the victim of a quaint old custom of chopping out the top panels and replacing them with uninspiring panes of glass. Here some research is necessary to determine what the old door was like and how it can be duplicated. This is a more important matter than it may seem off-hand, for the door is usually the dominating feature of the house. At least it contributes a great deal to the character of the façade.

When you have determined the age and the style—Chapter III should help you—the next step is to look over the stocks of secondhand lumber dealers or wreckers' yards, or watch for old-time houses being razed. Before actually buying a new door it is as well to check over the doorframe to see whether or not it has been made larger or higher. The lights above the door are a good indication, as is the presence of a new entablature. It was common practice to enlarge the doors when they were replaced, and to substitute a single door for a two-leaf door when stairs were changed and inside porches enlarged.

These are all major features to be corrected, but very often the charm and interest of an old house hang more on the small details than the large ones, especially in the interiors. An ugly mantel shelf or fancy crane, for instance, will quickly destroy the authentic appearance of a room. Hardware is another item that needs to be genuine. So many of the old houses have hinges and latches that are far more recent than the house itself. Indeed, after inspecting some hundreds of houses in various parts of the country, we are convinced that, somewhere between the Civil War and 1911, someone did an excellent selling, or trading, job in these commodities.

We find houses built in the 1700s with latches made after 1840, not on one or two doors, but throughout. We see similar doors with the nail or screw holes where HL hinges have been, but now hanging on cast-iron butts. It seems as though some despicable character had made a deliberate house-to-house hunt for old hardware, offering brand-new, up-to-date substitutes which the house owners could not resist. It is, of course, a well-known fact that empty houses are considered fair game for vandals posing as antiquarians, who strip them of every old-time fitting and fixture. Strangely enough these selfsame marauders would be horrified at the idea of being considered common thieves.

Inasmuch as one of the cardinal aims of restoration is to return a house to its original state, it is essential to use similar materials to those used, and preferably of the same age. This includes: wood for paneling, molding, door or window replacements, floor boards, sheathing for wainscoting or dados, fireplace mantels, cupboard doors, and beams for ceilings. Hardware would include: hinges, latches, shutter fasteners, knockers, and bolts. Glass for windows, and for sidelights around the front door if it is of that type. Plaster is the possible exception, as the modern method of making plaster is far more desirable, and the same effect may be obtained by proper application and finish.

Scouring the countryside for these materials may take a little time, but it will be worth it for all the fun you will have. It is quite an education rummaging about in junk yards or secondhand dealers' premises, and everyone knows what fun auctions are. Sometimes you can pick up enough paneling for an entire room at an auction. Then there are dealers with perfectly fascinating collections of used *old* materials—fences, doors, cupboards, hinges, window frames with the old glass still in them, old brick, beautifully carved mantelpieces, gates, and old pine or oak boards of every length and width. The storehouses of professional house wreckers sometimes contain a wealth of old material. Still another source of supply would be the purchase of an old barn, an old mill, or, if you are lucky, even an old house. Extra beams for the living-room ceiling might be found in an old tumble-down barn whose roof and sheathing are gone, but into whose beams rot or termites have not yet found their way.

# CHAPTER VI

# House Timbers

THE most amazing part of an Old Colonial is its frame—the heavy beams and posts that support even the tiniest, simplest old wooden house. When you consider the skilled workmanship and the time and effort expended in cutting out the huge timbers and putting them together, it is little wonder they have lasted for centuries and today constitute a splendid memorial to those early craftsmen who built for the generations to come.

In these braced-frame houses not more than a dozen vertical posts, some of them eight or ten inches square, support the floor beams and the roof, and the horizontal members that form a frame for the walls. Since the timbers for each wall were assembled flat on the ground, erecting such a house was a job that called for no little skill and a vast amount of brawn. No one man and his family could do it alone. It was a community job that usually became a social occasion, known to those who took part in it as a "raising bee."

For miles around the countryside whole families turned out for the "raisin'." To the men fell the task of hoisting the framework of their neighbor's new home into position. The women fed the hungry and thirsty workers after their strenuous job was done. No doubt the generous quantities of "flip" that were served added to the conviviality of the occasion.

But, before the neighbors arrived, much work had already been done. Not only must the cellar hole have been dug and the foundation laid, but every piece of timber required must have been cut, hewn or sawn, and laid on the ground in its proper order, ready for that exciting moment when it was needed.

While the women set to preparing quantities of filling food, the men busied themselves whittling dozens of hardwood pegs with which to lock the joints in place. Then came the assembling of the frames forming the front and back walls, as the timbers lay on the ground. The huge beams and posts were fitted together so that each side of the house could be raised in one piece. The corner and intermediate posts and the studs were framed into the big beams. With pod augers, holes were bored into which the wooden pegs would later go to secure the joints. And so in a few hours each broadside was completed, and all was ready for the main event—the actual raising!

Each man had his pike close at hand as the "breath-taking" moment arrived. These pikes were metal-tipped poles, sixteen feet long, with which they pushed the timbers upright and held them steady while others pegged them in position.

With the men standing shoulder to shoulder, the mighty task of lifting the heavy frames was begun. As the top came shoulder-high, the pikes were placed in position. Then, carefully and slowly, the huge structure was pushed upright on the sturdy underpinning, steadied by men on the other side to keep it from toppling too far. Other groups of husky workers quickly lifted the end girts with their pikes and tied the two walls together so that the frame would stand alone. And so the biggest job was done, and you may be sure that the call to dinner was a welcome intermission before the task of laying the roof timbers was begun.

This is the scene that comes to mind whenever we examine the frame of an old house. Although the frame is the least likely part of the house to have been disturbed, its construction and workmanship are, unfortunately, no sure guide to the date of erection. Nevertheless it does provide us with a certain amount of useful information.

The braced-frame type of construction followed the earlier half-timbered house of the seventeenth century. It, in turn, was superseded in the middle of the nineteenth century by the balloon type of frame.

In the braced-frame, the structure consists of a few very heavy timbers that support the roof, floors, and walls. In the balloon-frame, most of the wood pieces are of small size, but there are a great many of them. The basic timber today is the two-by-four. In the old houses it was something like eight-by-eight!

In the old days, when housebuilding was more or less of a community affair and the labor was a minor item, the braced frame had much to recommend it. Once in position, these great posts and beams were there to stay. And, generally being of oak, they became tougher with time and better able to resist the elements, termites, and fire. One old lady of our acquaintance owes her life to the flame-resisting qualities of this old oak. One night an oil drum afire in her cellar raged for hours before it was put out. But the oak beams and floor boards, though deeply charred, had kept the fire from spreading through the house. Old pine would, of course, have burned like tinder.

Some of the early brick houses were made with wood frames, the brick being used to fill in the walls. Later the wood frame was largely dispensed with and the brick walls made thick enough to carry the weight of the roof and floor timbers. In most of the small brick and stone houses of the eighteenth century, the horizontal timbers were large and heavy, and followed the same system as in the frame house.

White oak was the principal material used for house timbers, though pine was often used for floor joists, and black walnut was favored for ceiling beams in some parts of the Middle West. From the earliest days the large beams and posts were hewn by hand, usually with a broadax. The lighter timbers and boards were sawn, either by hand or by water power.

In either case the straight saw left its easily recognized imprint on the boards. It scored straight lines across the width of the board. If the work was done by hand the lines will be at a somewhat smaller angle to the edge of the boards than if a power saw was used. You can very easily tell the difference between these marks and those made by the circular saw, which was first used in 1814. The circular saw was

The pedimented gable and classical porch with columns—in this case Corinthian—are typical of the Greek Revival style, but more often the corner boards are replaced with wide pilasters. Veranda roofs on the ells are Victorian additions.

A substantial brick Georgian house in Delaware. Note twin end chimneys and captain's walk. Dropped Palladian window is unusual. Extra height and added dignity secured by raising main floor four feet from street level. (*Courtesy The New-York Historical Society, New York.*)

A New England Early American house with stone chimney top, built before 1750, its proportions ruined by added porches and dreary appendage at rear, and feeling of roof spoiled by tar-paper roofing over shingles.

A Southern Early American house of brick, with one external and one built-in end chimney. Extra doorways apparently were added later. Numerous houses of this type were built before 1770. (*Courtesy The New-York Historical Society, New York.*)

heavy and wobbled badly as it ran, making deep gashes in the wood. The marks were curved like the edge of the saw.

Sometimes you may come across boards that you can tell were cut by a handsaw because the sawmarks stop a few inches before the end of the board. The reason for this is that the ends of the wood rested on trestles, and it was much easier to split the end than to move the log so that the saw cut could be finished. The split end was then usually dressed with an ax or an adze.

Unlike the boards and planks, the beams and posts often consisted of a whole log. It was therefore much easier to trim them to shape with an ax than to shave off thin layers with a saw. So skilled did the old-time carpenters become in the use of the broadax and drawknife that they could trim a log perfectly smooth to any required dimensions. Consequently any exposed woodwork in a house frame was always finished smooth, and no toolmarks showed. The one exception was in cellar beams, which very often bear the mark of ax cuts.

Although house beams and posts were cut by hand as late as 1850, this rule prevailed, and only the parts that were hidden beneath plaster and panel were left in their rough, untrimmed state. Exposed ax-marked beams and posts, therefore, are not authentic, and the common practice of using old ax-marked barn timbers to replace rough ceiling joists is, to put it mildly, a mistake.

What did happen is that around 1750, when there were plenty of water-power sawmills turning out boards, the beams and posts were often cased in. These heavy timbers were then only given a rough trimming and enclosed with beautifully fitted and finished boards of pine, chestnut, or some other easily worked wood. In a later period the walls of a wooden house were made thicker so that the posts could be enclosed within them. Whenever the posts are exposed, if they are in a very rough condition, you can generally find the marks of the casing on the floor boards, and sometimes the ceiling. In any case the flooring will probably not fit tight against the post.

Since before 1700 all the smaller timbers were sawn, so long as they were exposed they were very carefully smoothed with a drawknife or a plane. But when they were enclosed in ceilings they were left rough. Some of them even had traces of the bark left on them. This can generally be taken as a clear indication that the ceiling was originally built that way, and exposed beams would not be authentic. If the plaster is removed, the ugly joists will certainly need to be replaced. Of course, anything may happen to a ceiling in 175 years or more. We have even found them made of "decorative" squares of tin nailed to the rough joists and painted over. In such a case something has to be done, and the new owner may well be excused for substituting a set of hand-finished beams. But even then, ax marks are taboo!

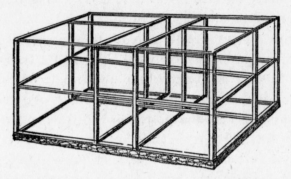

A twelve-post, braced frame, for a central-chimney
house.

Before planning alterations of any kind to the wooden structure, it is as well to know what you are likely to find regardless of the material of which the outer walls are composed. In the wooden house everything is supported by the frame which sits upon a stone or brick foundation. One of the simplest frames is that of the central-chimney-type Early American house. In a two-story house of this type there will be a post at each corner, the full two stories high. There will also be two intermediate posts, one each side of the chimney at the front and two corresponding posts at the back. These eight posts are tenoned into the horizontal sill which rests on the foundation and forms the base for the whole frame.

At the second-floor level each of the front posts will be connected to its mate at the rear by a beam called a girt—end girts at the gables and chimney girts on either side of the chimney. At the foundation level there will be only two girts, one each side of the chimney, which, in this case, are called cellar girts. Along the front and back of the house the posts are connected at the second-floor level by horizontal timbers called the front and rear girt respectively. At the roof level there is another set of end and chimney girts, but the front and rear

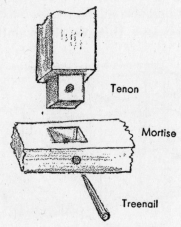

Tenon

Mortise

Treenail

How the timbers are joined in a
braced-frame house.

horizontal timbers that support the roof rafters are known as wall plates. Most of these timbers are mortised and tenoned together and the joints locked with pegs driven through them. In some cases other forms of joints, such as dovetails, are used.

In houses that have rooms behind the chimney, as in the case of a lean-to or any house two rooms deep, there will be another set of four posts. The end and chimney girts are tied into these. In such a house there would then be twelve posts, which is quite a common arrangement.

These main timbers of a house are usually far apart, and, since they did not use inside walls as bearing partitions, the joists would have to be quite heavy to span the distances involved without bending. To overcome this the old-time carpenters interposed another heavy beam called a summer beam to carry one end of the joists, which could then be made half as long.

If you are acquainted with old house structure at all, you doubtless have been introduced to the summer beam. But in case you have never met, this is the imposing beam that spans each front room of some Early American houses and the first of the Georgians from the chimney girt to the end girt. You will find summer beams chiefly in the ceiling of the first and second floors, paralleling the front of the house. If the house requires it, there might even be two summer beams

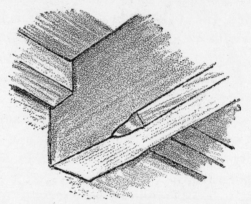

A chamfered summer beam supporting a joist.

on the first and on the second floors. These beams are readily recognized by their great size. Only in Massachusetts do the summer beams run in the opposite direction, that is, from the front of the house to the rear.

By 1725 in some sections the carpenters began leaving out the first-floor summer beams so that the whole ceiling could be plastered. This meant using much heavier joists, making the ceiling that much thicker. In other instances they reduced the height of the beam so that it could be enclosed in the ceiling. Its presence can sometimes be detected from the ridges in the plaster, or thin cracks that mark its lower edges. After 1750 they extended these practices to the second floor. In some of the earlier houses a summer beam is found in the cellar ceiling, but this is comparatively rare.

The timbers from which the braced frame gets its name are the diagonal braces between sills or girts and the posts. The number used depends on the individual design and is of little importance unless one happens to be in the way of some alteration you wish to make. Since they are largely responsible for keeping the walls vertical, they should never be removed or even cut into.

The external walls of the house are formed of vertical timbers to which a covering of some kind is applied. Most frequently these timbers consist of studs framed top and bottom into the girts and sills or girts and plates. The studs are usually $2 \times 3$ inches, or some odd size near that, set with the longest dimension parallel to the wall. They are spaced from 20 to 24 inches apart, from center to center. Modern $2 \times 4$ inch studs are much closer, usually 16 inches on centers.

You may occasionally encounter another type of wall construction consisting of $1\frac{1}{4}$- or $1\frac{1}{2}$-inch boards pegged to the frame. But these, like the studs, do not contribute much to the strength of the frame; their purpose is merely to form a point of attachment for the inner and outer wall coverings.

An interesting feature of the frames of some of the eighteenth-century houses is what is known as an overhang. This overhang is formed by the projection of an upper story beyond the wall below it. Overhang was common on seventeenth-century houses, being a survival from the English town houses. This extension of the second, and sometimes the third, floor was intended to provide shelter for the merchants' stalls erected below them in the narrow streets. It is not, as some romantic souls would have us believe, adapted from the blockhouse as a defense measure against Indian attacks!

This early overhang was provided by extending the upper part of the frame beyond the first-story posts and was called a framed overhang. By the eighteenth century, however, that type of overhang had disappeared. Its place was taken by an overhang of four or five inches, and even that had dwindled to a meager inch or so by the late seventeen hundreds. This vestigial overhang was secured by cutting away the posts below the second-floor level, so that they were narrower up to that point than they were above. For this reason it is referred to as the hewn overhang. There are quite a few old houses with this feature still in existence. The overhang may be confined to the front of the house or may extend around one end or even both. Sometimes a third floor overhangs a second, forming a double overhang. Overhang is a feature of the central-chimney house and is never encountered in those with central halls.

In brick and stone houses there is of course no need for vertical posts to hold up the wall covering and the floors. The timberwork therefore consists of horizontal beams and joists, whose ends are supported by the outside walls. Where there are end chimneys and a central hall, the floor framing will probably consist of heavy beams paralleling the chimneys, and one along each wall of the central hall. These two pairs of beams may each carry a summer beam or its equivalent, and sometimes two. The summers, however, will not cross the hall. This same construction is often used where the gables of the house are of stone or brick and the other two sides of wood. In these cases there would also be vertical posts to support the ends of the main-floor timbers, eight in all. The gables give no support, though the center part of one beam might be carried by the front of each chimney.

In checking over the main timbers of a house for restoration, there is probably little that will need attention except the sills, and perhaps the recasing of visible posts and beams. It is, however, a good idea to check the main posts and see that none has been cut away or weakened in any respect. We have in mind one instance where a corner post was entirely removed to a height of seven feet to accommodate a doorway to an outside porch! Why the corner of the building did not sag is a mystery to this day.

In many of the small houses the corner posts which show give character to a room. Such a post that has its original casing is quite as effective and much more authentic than the naked post. This fact is emphasized, because far too many amateur restorers strip off the casings which they consider later additions and stand back to admire the ax marks on the post which the builder went to such pains to hide.

In any house that has a cellar the sills can usually be felt, if not seen, on top of the foundation wall. The knife test should be used for rot and termites and every effort made to examine the wood visually. You should keep a sharp lookout for signs of powdered wood, for mold and other signs of deterioration and dampness. The nose is a good indicator of that last condition.

Quite probably it will not be possible to see the feet of the posts, but you may be able to get at the tops of some of them by exploring inside the roof. The plates should be inspected at the same time. A knife fastened to a stick is a useful instrument to take along, together with a good flashlight or extension lamp. Then you can dig into the plates—except on a story-and-a-half house—without getting so many cobwebs in your hair.

Any defects in the sills, posts, or plates call for the immediate attention of a capable carpenter or repairman, but not, it is to be hoped, the exterminator. This subject of posts and plates we can go into in greater detail after reviewing the more important items of roof construction and their relation to the frame, or walls, on which they rest.

# CHAPTER VII

# Rooftrees and Rafters

THE one timber of a house that poets grow sentimental over is the rooftree. It symbolizes the stanch protective quality of the roof. Yet a great many old and enduring houses have no rooftrees at all!

The rooftree, or ridgepole, is a timber that runs the full length of the ridge, and all rafters are framed into it. Usually, on our smaller houses it was made approximately square, perhaps 8 by 8 inches, and set so that one sharp corner formed the ridge. Such rooftrees were used here and there on the earliest houses, but in some districts they were more common during the second half of the eighteenth century. Their presence or absence, accordingly, is no indication of age.

The type of roof framing used is affected in a great degree by the kind of roof it is called upon to support. And the roofs of the Colonial houses, with their additions and modifications throughout the years, show a surprising diversity of style. There is the sharp-angled peak pitch, a hang-over from the seventeenth-century thatched roof which was excessively steep. With the adoption of shingles as a covering the need for the steep roof disappeared, but the style persisted for some time. As a rule, though, after 1700 the roofs became progressively flatter, the exact amount depending on the locality and the prevalence of snow or rainstorms. The peak roof thus became the low-pitched gable roof. An interesting variation of the pitched roof is that known as the rainbow roof. It is nothing more nor less than a pitched roof that is given a gentle upward curve, so that, from the gable ends, it seems slightly rounded.

When a single-story addition was made to the back of a pitched-roof house, the rear half of the roof came down low, forming the lean-to style of roof. If more room was needed in the pitched roof, the pitch was made very steep for a few feet up from the attic floor and then brought over to the ridge at an almost flat angle. This produced what is known as a gambrel roof, a name derived from the similarity between the shape of the rafters and a horse's hock. Two variations of

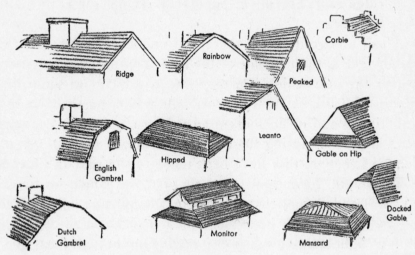

Some common types of early roofs.

this style of roof are known as the Dutch and the English gambrel, but so far as we can ascertain, the difference has never been technically defined. From comparative views of these roofs, the only discernible difference is that the Dutch type is lower in proportion to its width, so that the slope of its lower section is less steep than it is in the English type. All in all, it is a matter that need give us little concern.

Very few early small houses have hipped roofs, which are pitched roofs with their ridge cut short at both ends so that there are no gables. They may occasionally be seen on houses built after 1800, especially on the Georgian style. They are commoner on the larger houses, and the smaller ones that are surmounted by a "captain's walk"—or a "widow's walk," if your fancy turns more to the morbid than the romantic!

Where a lean-to extension is made to a hipped roof, the result is a gable-on-hip. This is found as infrequently as a monitor roof which sets out to be either a pitched or a hipped roof but has another roof sticking out on top of it. Small windows adorn the strip of wall that separates the two. From this it will be gathered that by far the commonest form of roof is the pitched roof, which is also called a gable roof or ridge roof. Second in popularity among the early builders was the gambrel.

On all of these old houses there will undoubtedly be some means of gaining access to the inside of the roof. Perhaps it is only a small trap door through which you may find it difficult to squeeze. But the effort will usually be well worth the while, particularly if you are thinking of adding dormers or an attic or making other important changes. While exploring these dim recesses you may also discover evidence of changes that have been made to the roof in times long past. You might, for instance, find that either a single- or two-story lean-to was added, and that the original house was only one room deep—and perhaps only one room wide!

With no light and on a sunny day, poking up through the trap door, or even climbing the old narrow stairs alongside the upper chimney, is a quick and sure way of finding leaks in the roof! To inspect the roof timbers, however, you will need a good light such as a hundred-watt bulb on the end of a heavy rubber-covered, fifty-foot extension cord. A necessary precaution, too often forgotten with disastrous results should there be no floor, is to rest your weight always on the beams or joists, and never on the laths and plaster between them!

The arrangement of the roof timbers that you find, and the details of its construction, will have been determined to a great extent by the local fashion and the date of erection. In roof structures there are many ways of doing the same thing, and it often seems that the carpenters were determined to use all of them. In the gable roof a popular form of framing consists solely of a series of common rafters spaced about three feet apart. These rafters, which are all of the same size, are jointed and pegged at the bottom to the wall plate, and each pair is fastened together at the top. On small houses one room deep there may be no other main timbers. But if the roof has to span two rooms (or one very wide one) the rafters may be stiffened by a horizontal beam connecting each pair about halfway up between plate and ridge. These beams are jointed into the rafters to keep them from bending inward under the weight of the roof covering. They also help to keep the rafter feet from spreading, and stiffen the whole structure.

Such rafters as we have examined have varied in size from $4\frac{1}{2} \times 5$ to 6 inches square, but there is no set standard. Neither is there any ruling to govern the finish of the roof timbers. Sometimes they are very carefully trimmed smooth with an ax; in other instances they are roughly cut tree trunks with the bark still on.

Since there is no ridgepole in this type of roof, and no other lengthwise timbers to connect the rafters, they are held in their relative positions by a layer of horizontal boarding nailed or pegged to them. This boarding covers the entire area from wall plate to ridge on both sides of the roof and forms the foundation for the shingles. The boards usually are very roughly sawn, and not trimmed along the edges, so that there are often wide gaps between them.

At the gables the space is usually filled in with vertical studs just as the house walls are, and the siding nailed to them. Strangely enough we have come across several examples, built just prior to or a little after 1776, in which the north or northeasterly gable was also plastered inside!

Another popular system of roof construction employs what are known as principal rafters. These are made heavier than the common rafters, and there are fewer of them. They are tied together by means of horizontal beams called purlins, which run the full length of the roof and are generally framed into the top side of the rafters so as to form a level surface to which roof sheathing can be nailed. On this kind of roof structure, the sheathing boards are placed parallel with the rafters and fastened to the purlins. Some roofs have only three or four large purlins to a side, and others have up to a dozen small ones. In the latter case they are often not framed into the rafters but simply

[ 91 ]

nailed or pegged on top of them. Usually one of the purlins forms a ridge.

Variations of these types of roof structure include a combination of principal and common rafters, which usually incorporates one heavy purlin on the underside of the rafters and collar beams on the principals. Also much used in some areas is a common-rafter system with a principal rafter at each end and on either side of a central

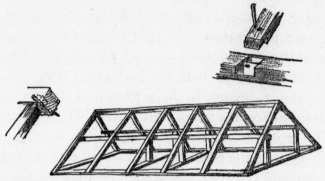

Framing and joints of a principal rafter roof with heavy purlins.

chimney. The single purlin may then consist of two end sections and a short center one, each of the three being braced by a diagonal piece from a principal rafter.

Theoretically, in the one-and-a-half-story house, the roof framing need be no different from that of the full two-story building. From the inside the only difference is that part of the ceiling is fastened to the rafters so that it slopes with them. The flat portion may then be hung from joists that are tied to the rafters some distance up from the wall plate. While this can be done in very small houses, where the roof span is insignificant, a much more complicated roof structure is usually called for. In a one-and-a-half-story house built in 1775, for example, we found heavy chimney girts in the attic floor. These terminated, not in the front and rear wall plates, but in beams parallel to the ridge which were, in effect, summer beams. These beams extended from the end girts to the chimney girts, where they joined

[ 92 ]

posts that stood on the first-floor chimney girts. These posts were carried on upward to form supports for a pair of heavy purlins, one to each roof slope. At each end, and between the chimney girts, the whole vertical structure was stiffened by heavy braces. Long joists between the summers and short ones between the chimney girts formed the attic-floor timbers and supported the ceilings of the rooms below. Other lighter timbers extended from the summers to the rafters to carry the rest of the lower ceiling.

At their top ends, the 4×5 inch rafters were mortised into a heavy 8×8 inch ridgepole, and pinned. The chief point of interest in such a roof is that the main-floor timbers are tremendously strong and supported at several points so that they could very well sustain a floor. Furthermore, the position of the heavy purlin and the spacing of the rafters would make possible the installation of small dormers, provided the side walls of the attic came down from the purlins. With the proper framing between the purlins and rafters it would even be possible to make space for a wide dormer by cutting out part of one rafter above the purlin. The rafter stumps would, of course, have to be properly supported by framing the opening with heavy timbers. Obviously roofs with collar beams above the floor level are not suitable for conversion into rooms, and heavy purlins should never be cut without competent advice.

It is, of course, quite impossible to describe in detail all the roof-member combinations that may be found, and if it were, the result would be deadly dull to all except architects and the technically minded. It is, however, necessary to discuss briefly the gambrel, which is one roof that offers possibilities for securing extra usable space—and is therefore most likely to be mistreated. Fortunately there is little variation in gambrel construction, and what differences there are probably will not interfere with the use of the space they provide.

The typical gambrel roof, then, is similar to the common-rafter pitched roof except that the lower part is at a much steeper angle. At the point where the pitch of the roof changes, there is a heavy purlin both front and back. The ends of these purlins are connected by shorter ones that extend across the gables. This purlin system is supported by massive purlin posts which stand on the four girts. Gambrel roofs on houses with end chimneys may be somewhat similar, but they are more likely to have a heavy truss framing at each end. There may also be a similar truss (of the king-post type) in the middle, with openings at the sides big enough to accommodate doorways. In such a case there would be space for at least two rooms occupying the whole length of the house.

Because of the clear space between the rafters, from wall plates to purlins, the insertion of dormers would be comparatively easy. Such dormers, however, need to be very carefully designed or the whole balance and feeling of the roof may be spoiled. It is the sad truth that a two-story house that is only one room deep wears a gambrel roof with a sheepish air, and dormers only make appearances worse! On the other hand, a gambrel spanning two rooms usually has better proportions and can carry dormers gracefully. But they must be of the proper size and located at the correct distance above the eaves line. It is all a matter of size and mass, and no problem for an amateur to decide.

Some of the gambrels are so high that there is ample space under the purlins for a room of usable height, plus a small attic above. There are quite a few examples with this arrangement built after 1750.

In checking over the roof timbers there is always the exciting possibility of finding evidences of early changes in the structure of the house. For example, the original house may have been one room deep, with a single-story lean-to. If, at some later date, the lean-to was increased to two stories, the roof timbers will probably tell the tale. Something of the sort may be suspected if the rear half of the roof is longer and at a flatter angle than the front half.

While it would be quite possible to extend the rear roof to cover the lean-to without disturbing the rest of the roof, it is more likely that the whole structure was rebuilt. You can usually tell what happened by examining the rear wall plate of the original part of the house. This will show the joints where the rafter feet were framed into it.

# Rooftrees and Rafters

The original end rafters, or even all of them, may still be in position, with the new ones on top of them and extending rearward at a flatter angle. More often than this, the lean-to was built up only high enough to permit the extension of the old rafters to cover it. The extra lengths of rafter then will be seen attached to the lower end of the original ones.

In other cases the ends of the original rafters may have been raised a couple of feet by means of a beam supported that distance above the wall plate. If the whole roof had been altered to keep it symmetrical, the ridge will, of course, have been moved backward. The chimney, or chimneys, will then be either astride the ridge or in front of it. This possibility has to be taken into account in judging the age of the house by the relation of the chimney to the roof ridge. In central-chimney houses, it will be recalled, the older houses often had the chimney behind the ridge.

Another interesting piece of history may be uncovered in a house of Dutch origin (or one built by a carpenter whose mother was frightened by a Dutchman). Such houses often had roofs that swept down into a curve at the eaves. In later times this curve may have been straightened out, as it has been in several notable old houses. The evidence of this not-altogether-happy change may be found in the straight lengths of rafters pinned to the original ones above the jointed section that forms the curve. The upper half of the joint, complete with peg holes, may very well remain. If that is so, restoring the original Dutch roof lines is a comparatively simple matter, though it may not be advisable because of the porch or room extension now under the eaves, for the accommodation of which the change was made.

Not so interesting as ferreting out changes, but much more important, is checking the roof for defects. You can make a good start in this direction by looking the roof over from the outside, to see whether or not it is level or if it sags.

A sagging roof, like a sway-backed horse, is not pretty. Whether it is serious or not depends upon the cause. In wooden houses that have settled, the wall plates may be slightly bowed, causing the rafters to sink at one or more points. This, in turn, drops the ridge. Another cause may be the sagging of rafters due to warping, especially where there are no collar beams. Sometimes a ridgepole will sag with age, particularly if it has become damp through a prolonged roof leak. In central-chimney houses where the ends of two halves of a ridgepole rest on the chimney, they may drop through perishing of the bricks or crumbling of the stone, or even the rotting of the ends of the wood. Most of these things can be corrected or disguised unless there is some defect in the timbers or the supporting structure.

In the case of rotted rafters or purlins the obvious remedy is replacement. Sometimes the rotted part can be cut out and the gap braced by equally strong pieces bolted or pegged on both sides of the break. If it is the wall plate that is gone, it will have to be replaced and the rafter feet framed into the new member, provided the feet also are not rotted! The principle to be followed in all such cases is to replace any timber with one of the same dimensions and strength. Putting in a weaker timber merely transfers some of the stress to the rest of the structure and may result in the failure of another part.

By far the most serious cause of a sagging roof is the bulging of the house walls. This generally results from a weakness in the house frame, or the outward settling of stone or brick walls or foundations. The crumbling of a rotten sill may have the same effect. Correcting these things is a major operation, if it can be done at all. Tie rods may help in some cases.

Thus we come to the subject of roof coverings, which is a far more important matter than many a modern specimen of domestic architecture would suggest. Here the unenlightened urge to treat an old house as something frivolous and "cute" too often becomes irresistible, particularly in the case of the summer residence. And in their misguided impulses the house owners are aided and abetted by manufacturers and dealers who urge upon them the colorful but hideous substitutes for the dignified shingles they were designed to wear. Especially does this occur where the house happens to be in or near a

A random stone house built by the Huguenots in New York State in 1705. Note terne-plate roof and solid shutters. Double-decked porch appears to be a later addition. (*Courtesy The New-York Historical Society, New York.*)

A pair of Dutch "kicks" to a terne-plate roof on Long Island. The fancy porch and lean-to are out of character. (*Courtesy The New-York Historical Society, New York.*)

A typical early eighteenth-century Connecticut saltbox with oddly spaced gable windows and unpainted clapboards. The gable has a slight overhang, and the door hood is an addition. (*Courtesy The New-York Historical Society, New York.*)

A Southern English-gambrel type house in North Carolina. House is of wood with brick foundation and end chimneys. Porch is a later addition. (*Courtesy The New-York Historical Society, New York.*)

modern housing development in which traditional houses are reproduced in a miniature scale, with doormat-sized lawns, solid shutters pierced with quaint designs like the door of a privy, startling colors, and mock street lamps on white posts at the midget garden gates. These doll houses are, in all probability, capped with flagrantly asbestos shingles in gay blues and mottled reds. And the disease is contagious.

Colored shingles of any kind on an eighteenth-century house are an anachronism, and the greatest sinners in this respect are the old-time property owners themselves. One of these descendants of the original builder thus outraged one of the few really unspoiled houses we have ever seen. It was an Early American with a stone central chimney, dating back at least two hundred years. The old windows were there, their tiny panes flush with the heavy muntins, and the trim flush with the siding. It was all there—yellow clapboards, white trim, light gray chimney, and—horror of horrors!—patent "tar-paper" shingles of a particularly nauseating shade of green!

It reminded us of a little house we had bought some time before, just because it seemed to need a friend. The owner had contracted for a new roof of asbestos shingles of a delicate shade of blue. Happily a ten-dollar bill secured a reprieve, the order was canceled, and we breathed again. Not that we have anything against asbestos shingles, per se. But they are modern, and there is no possible way of disguising the fact from the observing eye. They should be reserved for modern buildings. They can never look old, and the minute we use them the house loses part of its old-time atmosphere. The effect is that of a modern silk hat on a head that should be wearing the old-fashioned beaver. The only wear for a house that was born with wood shingles is shingles of wood!

The only valid objection to wooden shingles that we have heard is that they increase the insurance rates because of their flammability. In some places, and in some degree, this is doubtless true. But two things must be taken into account. One is that while the cost in insurance may be higher, it is probably worth it to own a house that has no jarring note to mar its exterior, and, two, that the fire objection can be largely overcome by chemical treatment of the shingles, or by the installation of a sprinkler system that operates outside the roof. A perforated water-distribution pipe hidden under the ridge boards will do the trick, and the roof soaked by the mere turning of a valve. We also have to remember that there are many other ways of making our homes safe from fire, some of them far more effective than using asbestos shingles. But a house of concrete, with nary a vestige of wood or fabric or other combustible substance, would be a cage—or a mausoleum.

It all resolves itself into a question of values; what we want out of life and the place we live in. And it might as well be admitted here that the choice of the kind of house to make into a home is a part of our philosophy, an expression of our attitudes and beliefs, and the balance we strike in our estimate of values. There should be no jarring, untrue note. That is why it is worth some little compromise; why the satisfaction of an honest house is worth a fire extinguisher on every floor with a couple of spares besides.

Shingles can be of various sizes and textures. They may be of pine, cedar, hemlock, spruce, or cypress, and they may be sawn or hand-split. The sawn shingle cannot equal the handmade in appearance. The individual handmade shingles are uneven, and their suface is rough, so that they cast interesting shadows. They have character, each being different from the rest, and the roof they form has a beauty that no other roof covering can surpass. In the old days they were split from a log by means of a knife-edged tool called a froe, which was struck on the back of the blade with a heavy mallet or "beetle."

Splitting the log lengthwise in quarters, eighths, sixteenths, and so on, produced shingles that tapered from a thick butt to a thin edge. They were trimmed with a drawknife on a shingle horse so that the outside was more regular than the inner side. Sometimes the finished butt was three quarters of an inch thick! The shingles were about the same size as those we use today, and sometimes larger. But often, besides being nailed at the top, they were fastened down at the bottom also, either by nails or wooden pegs. Today we are content with two nails halfway to the top. Modern shingles are sold by the square, which is one hundred square feet of finished roof, and this simplifies calculation. Most shingles today are sawn and smooth-surfaced. But hand-split ones can be obtained, though the cost is comparatively high.

If your old house needs reshingling, the new shingles can usually be installed on the old boards, unless the boards are rotted. In this process you will note that the boards are spaced several inches apart. This space increases both the life of the boards and the shingles by allowing air to get between them so that they can dry out quickly after rain. But, before reshingling, it is as well to check the condition of the roof timbers and have rotted rafters replaced. If a roof is slightly uneven in spots, the expert shingler can usually hide the depression by doubling up or otherwise packing his shingles. Naturally it is of no use doing that if there is something wrong with the rafter underneath. The most likely spot for rot to set in is where there have been leaks, and leaks frequently occur around chimneys, especially very old ones that are innocent of flashing. Instead of flashing there may be a course of projecting bricks or stones just clear of the ridge to deflect rain water from the joint. Flashing should always be installed, but as inconspicuously as possible. And the projecting course should not be cut away to do it.

It takes time for new shingles to weather and darken. The process can be hastened by dipping them before they are laid. Creosote or an oil stain can be used, and some mix paint with the creosote to get an antique effect, but this has to be carefully done or the method will be obvious and the results harsh. It is better to let the shingles age naturally rather than to give them an obviously artificial patina.

Not all old houses are roofed with shingles. Slate and tiles have been used in localities where they were available. Slate is sometimes found on houses in Pennsylvania and parts of New York State. Occasional slate roofs also occur in the Boston area. Tiles were used very early in Virginia and New Jersey and certain parts of Long Island.

Both of these roofings call for much heavier roof timbers than do the humble shingles.

Still another roofing used in the late eighteenth and early nineteenth centuries was terneplate, principally on brick and stone houses. Although it is less common on the smaller wooden houses, we have seen it used in New York State on the rear half of an 1820 roof that was shingled in front, and on the main roof of a house in southern Ohio, dating from 1830. The terneplate consists of iron or steel sheet coated with an alloy of four parts of lead to one of tin. It was practically

An old-style wooden gutter
and leader.

always laid in long strips parallel with the rafters, and with standing seams, i.e., the edges of each plate were turned up and soldered to the next one. Since most of this material was made in Wales, it must have been fairly expensive by the time it reached American roofs. The material was usually painted, and, having little eye appeal or architectural value, was employed principally on the flatter roofs, where it was not so noticeable. On roofs of small pitch it would undoubtedly be more efficient in excluding the weather than shingles. Apart from this there certainly would be little point to using it today.

Besides the covering, other features of the roof that effect its character and appearance are the methods of finishing off the eaves and the gable ends of the pitched roofs. On the early houses the roof did not overhang the gables. Instead it was finished off with flat boards called rakes that covered the end rafters. Often the rake was formed with a simple molding, which, in some instances, became more and more elaborate as time went on and the classical influences in architecture made themselves felt. In restoring Early American types of houses the original simplicity should be maintained.

In very many houses which represent the transition from the Early American to the classic styles, one of the first innovations was the extension of the roof beyond the gables. In the Georgian and Greek Revival houses this decorated overhang became a cornice, the counterpart of the one which was formed out of the projecting eaves.

Rain gutters were not used on Early American houses and were rare on any other kind till after 1800. Still there are some notable exceptions. On one brick house built in 1756 there was a hollowed wooden gutter molded on the front to form a cornice. But it has never been fully established that this was original.

After 1800 some of the classical houses were supplied with wooden gutters and leaders. Often simple gutters, made from two boards nailed together at right angles, were added to Early American houses at this time. These were the first of the hanging type of gutter and were supported by iron brackets driven into the wall plate. The leaders usually were square, being made of four boards. Gutters of white cedar have been known to last well over a century. Such gutters are much better-looking than the modern galvanized ones, and in every way more suitable for use on old houses. At least they will not rust and stain the woodwork, but they need to be kept painted both inside and out!

# CHAPTER VIII

# Walls—Inside and Out

THE materials that the old-time builders used for the outside walls of a small house was largely a matter of geography and personal taste. Stone, brick, or wood was used, depending upon which was most readily available and the kind of house the prospective owner desired. Local beliefs and superstitions also played their part, as in the case of one of the first small brick houses in New England. This was a house built in Salem in 1707. Because of the spreading rumor that brick houses were damp and unhealthy, this house was pulled down shortly after its erection and a wooden one substituted. As a result of such fantastic notions very few brick houses at all were built in the northern colonies before 1750. In other sections both brick and stone houses were erected in large numbers, and wooden houses were put up with brick or stone gable walls, usually with the fireplaces incorporated in them.

The Dutch were particularly partial to stone end walls and wooden gables. In the South bricks were favored for the larger houses from the earliest days. Since bricks, which were made in Virginia from 1611 on (1640 in New England), were available in substantial quantities after 1700, they were frequently used for the smaller houses of that time. Of course, bricks alone would not suffice. There also had to be available large quantities of lime with which to make mortar. Absence of this commodity, or the expense of transporting it, actually delayed the building of brick and stone houses in some sections for a good many years.

# Walls—Inside and Out

A great deal of research has been done on bricks, largely with the idea of establishing dates from their sizes. The net result seems to be that there never was any set standard. One man made them a little bigger or a little smaller than another. We have seen bricks made around 1700 which varied in dimensions from $1\frac{5}{8}$ inches to $2\frac{3}{8}$ inches thick, $6\frac{1}{2}$ inches to $8\frac{3}{8}$ inches long, and $2\frac{7}{8}$ inches to $4\frac{1}{4}$ inches broad. Other bricks made after 1775 ranged in size from 2 to $2\frac{1}{2}$ inches thick, $7\frac{3}{4}$ inches to $10\frac{1}{2}$ inches long, and $3\frac{7}{8}$ inches to $4\frac{3}{8}$ inches broad. Modern bricks are usually about $8 \times 3\frac{1}{2} \times 2\frac{1}{4}$ inches.

The color of the brick also varied considerably, but with more reason. In Maryland and Virginia, for instance, the natural clay made hard bricks of a deep red. In the Connecticut River Valley, the well-baked bricks were of a delightful pink color. In both cases the exact shade of color depended largely upon the degree of burning they underwent.

Bricks made during the eighteenth and early nineteenth centuries were rough in texture and uneven in shape. In the kilns some of them were not baked sufficiently and others were burned too much and became glazed. These variations in color and finish added to the attractive appearance of the old brickwork. Quite often the burned bricks with their bluish glaze were used to form interesting patterns. The bricklayer, like his brother artisan the carpenter, appears to have experimented with details, incorporating herringbone patterns in gables, projecting courses in walls and chimneys, and dogtooth designs in cornices, etc. The system that was used in laying the bricks, i.e., the bonding, also affected the character of the walls.

Bonding was achieved by laying some bricks lengthwise (stretchers), and others crosswise (headers). The two principal bonding systems used in the early days were the Flemish bond and the English bond. In the Flemish bond each course was laid with alternate headers and stretchers. A header in one course would be next to a stretcher of the course above and below it, thus making a two-way bond. The English bond consisted of alternate courses of headers and stretchers, also bonded vertically as in the Flemish bond. Much laιer the American bond was developed. This consisted of one course of headers for each five or six courses of stretchers. Individual masons introduced their own variations and sometimes mixed their bonds indiscriminately. One common trick was to form patterns or accentuate certain courses by using darkly burned bricks, generally headers, at regular intervals. This, however, is mere decoration, and has no special significance as to date or locality.

Flemish Bond

English Bond

Bonds in brickwork.

The use of headers of course indicates that the walls were at least two bricks thick—seven to eleven inches. This was quite heavy enough in a two- or two-and-a-half-story house to support the roof and floor timbers without the need for any vertical wood framing, but many were made much thicker. The beams were either let into the walls the distance of one brick, or supported on corbels. In many cases the main timbers were also carried on the chimneys where the brickwork was more substantial. There are still standing in various parts of the country houses with wooden frames filled in with brick. This brick may be either sun-dried or lightly burned clay which is soft, or hard-burned brick. In the former case the bricks were probably laid dry (i.e., without mortar), but the hard ones would more likely be set in clay or even lime mortar. Both would serve merely as insulation and carry no part of the wall load. The outer covering would be of wood.

In several parts of the country we have come across examples of brick facing used over wood-covered walls. The idea here, apparently, was to secure the added protection of brick against the weather. Presumably the brick facing was added long after the house was built. Possibly brick was not so readily available at the time of building, as often happened with the earlier houses. Usually, we find, it is quite impossible to determine dates and motives in connection with such changes. But we did learn the true history of one particularly fascinating example of brick facing over clapboards.

The house in question was L-shaped, with the main gable facing the highway. The main gable end and the projecting gable of the rear building which formed the ell were faced with light brick. The rest of the house was clapboarded. The striking feature of the pedimented main gable was the four slender white pilasters that reached from the base to the cornice. Inquiry revealed that the rear part of the house, minus the brick facing, had been built in 1780. The front portion of the building was added in 1815, hence the gable end pediment. The house was bought in 1830 by a gentleman who did not consider its appearance sufficiently impressive. He therefore instructed the local carpenter to do what he could to make it look more like a mansion. The brickwork and the pilasters were the result. Although the details and the execution would make an architect wince, the general effect of the white woodwork and the pink brick is delightful.

Both field stone and quarried stone have been used extensively for house walls. In the Early American houses the stones usually were left rough and set at random, often with wide joints that had to be filled in with mortar. In the Georgian style of house the walls were more likely to be of dressed stone (squared and smoothed), set in regular, even courses. Occasionally a different stone was used for contrast in the trim of the house. Sometimes the front of the house would be of dressed stone while the sides and back were of rubble.

In New England and New York both field stone and quarried stone were used on outside walls. Sometimes a house will have walls of stone and trim of brick. Examples of this are found both in New York and in Virginia. The Dutch settlers in New York, along the Hudson River and in the Genesee Valley, used stone for their walls, and in New Jersey they made effective use of the red sandstone common to that area by pointing up the joints with white mortar.

In Pennsylvania the field-stone walls characteristic of that section of the country are particularly good, thanks to the Welsh and English masons who settled there in the early days of the colony. Today the descendants of these masons carry on the traditions of their forbears, and so individual is their work that they are often in demand in distant parts of the country.

Occasionally you may come across brick or stone walls covered with stucco. This may not be so recent an addition as you may be inclined to think. Stucco is said to have been used by the Indians in the fifteenth century, but there is some doubt as to whether it was of the same composition as that used by the white men (probably lime and sand). At any rate stucco was used on early houses in the South, and to a lesser degree by the Dutch in New Jersey, New York, and Delaware. The Germans also used it in Pennsylvania. It has the advantage of providing extra insulation and protection against the elements. If your house should already have a coating of old stucco, there is probably little point to removing it.

In making restorations or additions to old stone or brick walls, it goes without saying that the original should be copied as closely as possible. Old bricks are generally available from demolished buildings, or you may be able, as we once did, to buy the chimney of an eighteenth-century house that has burned down or fallen into decay. Such bricks are easily cleaned because of the soft nature of the mortar. Likewise the old stone, nicely weathered, may sometimes be salvaged from old foundations, cellar holes, or chimneys. Such brick and stone, incidentally, make charming old-fashioned garden walls and walks.

In reproducing walls much of the original character is lost unless the old-style mortar is used. This was made of lime and sand only.

The addition of cement, which was not invented till 1875, spoils the color. If extra strength is needed, a cement mortar can be used for the construction and the joints later pointed with lime mortar.

By far the great majority of the small old-time houses still existing in America are of wood construction. And most of these have clapboards for their outer covering. Clapboards, which are now pretty well an American institution, were used in many parts long before 1700. The earliest ones were made of riven oak, split like shingles from logs four to six feet long. By 1700 most clapboards were sawn. The earliest of the sawn oak clapboards were not tapered (beveled), but were of an even thickness just like any ordinary board. In some instances they were given a decorative bead along the lower edge. But the use of oak was soon discontinued in favor of white pine or hard pine (sometimes tamarack), cedar, whitewood, or cypress. These withstood the weather better.

The typical clapboard then was $\frac{3}{8}$ to $\frac{5}{8}$ inches thick at the butt, tapering to a feather edge and smoothed on one side by planing. In the southern colonies it was often nine to ten inches wide, but elsewhere it was generally narrower. The clapboards were nailed to the studs, with the ends of each board cut at an angle so that they overlapped for about an inch and made a weather-tight joint. At the corners of the building they were fitted tight against corner boards. These corner boards, which vary from three to six inches wide, are an authentic mark of the Old Colonial. Clapboards should never be mitered to one another at the corners of the house, as is so often done on modern imitations of the early houses.

The wide clapboards used in the warmer climates overlapped one another vertically so as to leave about eight inches of the width of each board exposed to the weather. In the colder areas the lap was greater and the exposure less. But we cannot generalize even about this; there are too many exceptions. We have seen in New England a large number of houses with very old clapboards that have an exposure of seven and a half inches out of a total width of less than nine inches. On the other hand it was quite a common practice in the North

—after 1750—to graduate the exposure. For example, the width of the exposed board at the foundation might be two and a half inches, the next one two and five eighths, and the third two and three quarters, and so on till the maximum exposure was reached toward the top of the wall. Sometimes this was done by using successively wider clapboards, but more often they were of the same width and only the exposure varied. The reason for this graduated exposure is not clear, the explanation most often advanced being that it gives greater protection where it is needed most. But this is open to question, since in many cases the amount of lap remains the same throughout! The most logical supposition is that it added to the appearance.

On later houses the width of the clapboards was often reduced to six inches or less, with an exposure of four to four and a half inches. In the South the wider exposure (six to eight inches) remained standard practice.

In certain parts of New England, particularly in Rhode Island and Connecticut, boards were used for the sides of frame houses in place of studding. These are called plank-frame houses, and the planks are of oak, one and a half to two inches thick. They are pegged to the sills, which are rabbeted to receive them, and to the girts and plates. Usually they fit close together, but sometimes there is a space between them which may or may not be plugged with clay. The clapboards are nailed to these planks, making a much tighter wall than the studs would do.

Where clapboards have a beveled overlapping joint between their ends, one nail at this joint is sufficient to hold both. The boards above and below are arranged so that their joint comes elsewhere, and no two of them are in line. Another nail in the bottom of the overlapping board goes through the top of the next lower clapboard. In this way there are two nails to each clapboard joint, but it looks as if there were only one. It was common practice before 1800 to use handmade nails with larger heads for this work, and the result was quite decorative.

While this method of jointing and nailing was quite usual, we have examined a number of houses built in the last quarter of the eighteenth century which have butt joints and concealed nails. Some of these houses had clapboards that were not tapered but were the same thickness throughout.

Not all wooden houses were faced with clapboards. Another board facing that might well be mistaken for clapboarding is what is known as weatherboarding. This is found on houses built in 1710, but seemingly it did not become popular until half a century later. The weatherboards are flat boards, usually a little less than an inch thick

Details of: matched boarding, weather boarding; shingles; and clapboarding.

and ten to twelve inches wide. They are beaded on the lower edge, and the top edge is rabbeted to receive the board above it. The finished siding therefore has the appearance of thin clapboards, but the shadow is strengthened by the line of the bead. The bead serves no purpose other than to give the finished wall a more decorative and interesting appearance.

In all of these wood surfaces, especially when they are painted white, shadows of various kinds have architectural value. This is particularly noticeable in still another form of siding composed of matched boarding which has a very wide, tapering joint. The joint is a form of tongue and groove, but a wide space is left between the beginning of the tapered tongue and the end of the adjoining board.

One important advantage of this siding was that the boards could be nailed flat to the studs so that they would not curl, as wide clapboards sometimes do.

This type of siding, together with the beaded clapboards, was much used in Georgian-style houses because of the shadow effect. In contrast with both of these is the flat matched boarding, used between 1800 and 1820, where a plain background was needed to accentuate other decorative features, as in Greek Revival houses. Often the boards were six to eight inches wide and had tongue-and-groove joints with a bead. It was also a regular practice to use these boards on the front of the house only and cover the rest of it with clapboards.

Argument has long raged as to whether shingles or clapboards were first used for covering house walls. On the basis of the evidence we have been able to gather, it seems that the clapboards were the first to be used in most of the colonies. By the year 1700 there were a great many houses with clapboards and a great many with shingles and no insignificant number with both. That the clapboards were considered a more desirable finish is indicated by the fact that many houses had clapboards on the front and shingles elsewhere.

As may be expected, there were a number of exceptions to the rule. In some districts, such as the southwestern part of Connecticut, white pine, oak, cedar, or chestnut shingles (or shakes) were used from the earliest days. These shingles varied in width from six to ten inches, and in length from thirty to thirty-six inches. The butts were a half to three quarters of an inch thick, and the shingles were laid with anywhere from eight to sixteen inches exposed. For almost all the Colonial period the shingles were hand-split and finished with a drawknife on one side. As a rule they were of uniform width, but some of them were curved at the butt end. They were nailed, top and bottom, either to rough boards, usually oak, laid across the studs, as in the case of roofs, or to vertical plank siding that took the place of studs.

Normally the shingles were laid in parallel rows, the upper row lapping over that below it. In some parts of Pennsylvania, however, the shingles overlapped each other at the sides too. As in the case of clapboards, the shingles usually terminated against corner boards, but in some instances they were mitered together at the corners. Mitering of shingles may therefore be authentic though rare, while the mitering of clapboards is not.

Until 1770 or thereabouts most siding shingles were left in their natural state, but even in the early days it was quite usual to white-wash them. In the nineteenth century, and even in the twentieth, owners have been known to cover shingled walls with clapboards, and clapboards with shingles to make them weather-tight. It is always a good idea to check this by examining the walls either from the inside

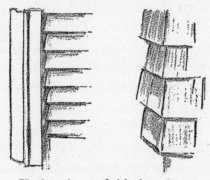

Clapboards are finished against a corner board. Shingles may be mitered.

or the outside. An attic gable is usually a good place to observe the kind of covering that has been applied to the studs or boarding. Shingled walls should always be stripped before new shingles are applied, and of course the original size and style of shingle should be reproduced. The preserving and aging of wall shingles is done in the same manner as those used for roofs.

## Interior Walls

In braced-frame houses it is rare to find a wall that carries the weight of anything above it. This usually happens only when some change has been made in later times and something added that was not in the original structure. The frame of the house normally supports everything within it, and the brickwork or stonework, such as a chimney or gable ends, helps.

In brick and stone houses built before 1826 the same thing applies. It is therefore usually quite a simple matter to move or eliminate a wall. But you have to be careful to ensure that you are really dealing with an interior wall. Sometimes what were originally outside walls are now inside because of additions that have been made. Then you may have an extra post in between the back lean-to post and the front post. This would be the main-house corner post, and removing it might well duplicate the disastrous feat of Samson pulling down the temple on his head.

The two kinds of interior walls commonly found are the stud type and the board-and-plaster type. When studs are used, the wall is exactly the same as a modern one, but the studs will be placed a few inches farther apart. Nailed to each side of the studs will be lathing to which plaster has been applied. In the very early houses this lathing was often made by splitting very thin boards (up to a quarter-inch thick) from a hemlock plank or log. These thin pieces were then hacked, and stretched sideways so that they split in several places along the grain. The whole thing was then nailed to the studs with the splits horizontal. Each piece was in this way made to serve the purpose of several laths. A little later the fashion swung to separate laths, still made of split hemlock, or of oak if that was not available, about two inches wide and forty or sixty inches long so as to nail to two or three studs. These laths were very rough and irregular, so that they formed a good key for the plaster, but the spaces between them varied greatly and there were intervals where the spaces were too narrow for the plaster to form a bond at all. Plaster was therefore likely to fall away in chunks.

The stud wall, then, consists of studs, usually two or two and a half inches by three, with lathing on both the three-inch sides. This produces a wall consisting of a layer of plaster and lath, an air space of two or two and a half inches, and another layer of lath and plaster.

# Walls—Inside and Out

If necessary, small pipes and an electric cable (BX) can be run inside such a wall. If there is a wooden baseboard, electrical outlets can be set into it.

These things are not possible with a board-and-plaster wall because there is no hollow space inside. The board-and-plaster wall is made of three-quarter-inch, seven-eighths-, or one-inch-thick boards. These form, as a rule, an almost continuous surface to which the laths were nailed and the plaster applied. The boards were rough-sawn,

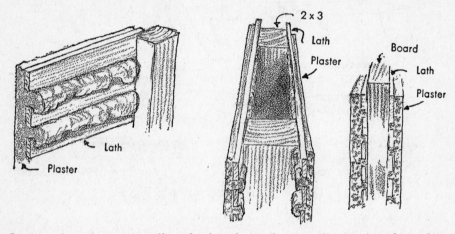

Sections through a stud wall, and a board-and-plaster wall, showing plaster key.

sometimes with the edges trimmed square and sometimes left irregular. Normally they would be twelve to twenty inches wide and spaced not more than an inch or so apart. An exception might be a partition separating a room from a cellar or attic stairway. In such locations the boards are often no more than six inches wide and spaced six or eight inches apart. Normally there would be lathing on only one side, but the back of the partition would be plastered in between the boards. This back plaster would be sunken or hollowed in between the boards, and level with their back surface only at the edges.

The manner in which the studs and boards are fastened at floor and ceiling seems to vary from house to house rather than according to locality. It might also depend on whether or not the partition was installed after the flooring had been laid. We have seen instances of the studs being toenailed to the beams or joists, above and below, and others where they were nailed over the floorboards. The same thing applies to the board partitions. In other examples these boards have been held loosely in slots formed by two joists placed close together. When the lathing and plaster were removed it was easy to tilt the boards sideways and lift them out.

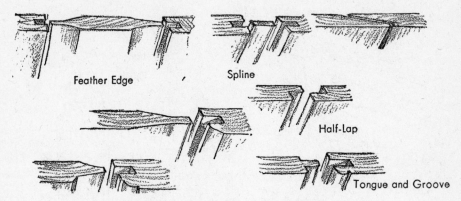

Types of joints used in wall paneling.

The important thing from the standpoint of remodeling, of course, is that either the stud or board walls can be removed easily without bringing down the house. And they can just as easily be installed elsewhere. The difficulty lies in adapting either of them to the accommodation of hot-air conduits or hot-water pipes, or using the board wall to hide anything at all. Often the only thing that can be done is to put up a second partition spaced from the original one by the amount of room required for this work. Otherwise it is necessary to box in the pipes and ducts. This boxing is best unless several such enclosures are called for in one wall, and usually they can be made to look as though they enclosed a beam.

In places where walls were not justified simple board partitions were used, and these often form some of the most interesting woodwork of the house. The boards are practically always placed vertically and extend from floor to ceiling. Usually they are at least a foot wide and may be of pine, chestnut, or even butternut. Sometimes the boards have square edges, but ordinarily they have some kind of joint that will seal the cracks. In very early partitions the boards will have a feather-edge joint, usually plain. To make this joint one board has both its edges tapered off in a long chamfer. The boards on either side of it will have a corresponding groove in each edge. In other cases the joints will be the familiar loose tongue, or the later tongue and groove.

# CHAPTER IX

# Doos and Doorways

OLD-TIME doors were something more than a convenient means of plugging a hole in the wall. The outside door, for example, not only kept out the wind and the rain, but animals, Indians, witches, and, it is whispered, even the Devil himself. Special designs of inside doors also were invested with magic properties. Though superstition has faded, the names remain to remind us of those disquieted days of ha'nts and evil spirits. Outside doors were usually of particularly heavy construction, even though the latchstring may have been left

The construction of a batten door.

[ 116 ]

out most of the time. The old hinges and ironwork were massive, and the bolts and bars plentiful and solid.

The earliest types of doors, after 1700, were the batten style for interiors and sheathed or lined doors for the exterior. On small houses paneled doors came in later.

The batten doors were made of two or three vertical boards, ¾ to 1¼

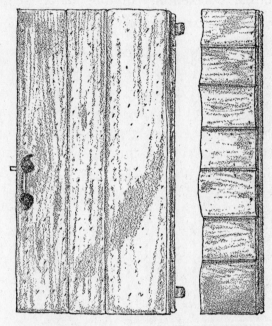

A sheathed door with horizontal lining boards.

inches thick, held together by two or three widely spaced horizontal boards, called battens, on the back. The vertical boards were often a foot or two feet wide and generally were half-lapped or splined together. The battens were either chamfered at all four edges or beaded on the long edges and attached to the vertical boards by handmade nails. More often than not these nails were driven in from the batten side and clinched over on the front side of the door, a rather untidy but effective practice.

Outside doors were, of course, much heavier than the inside ones.

Instead of using single planks, such as were common in the seventeenth century, the eighteenth-century carpenters favored the double-layer construction. Two boards thick, these doors were made in a variety of ways. In some the front layer was composed of one-inch boards, ten or eleven inches wide, placed vertically. The boards which formed the inner layer usually were somewhat narrower and thinner and arranged either horizontally or diagonally. In both layers the

An interior paneled door with raised panels.

boards occasionally had a formed joint of some kind, perhaps a plain overlap or a splined (loose-tongue) joint, or, in later examples, a more modern tongue-and-groove joint.

In many examples that we have seen, both the outer and inner boards were plain-edged, and one edge of each inner board was beaded. The two layers were fastened together with handmade nails, generally applied from the outside and clinched on the inside. Sometimes the nails were arranged to form a regular pattern all over the door. More ambitious carpenters used special nails with oversized heads that gave the effect of studs. These doors were known as lined or tomahawk doors.

No one seems to be able to date the appearance of the panel door accurately, but it is evident that they were very early. The simplest type, for interior use, consisted of a thin frame, often only seven eighths of an inch thick, with panels that were flush on the front and sunk slightly on the back. The frame consisted of top and bottom rails with stiles forming the sides. The number of intermediate rails and stiles depended upon the number of panels. Stiles and rails were mortised and tenoned together and then pinned with small wood pegs. In this way a stiff frame was formed which would not shrink as a layer of plain boards or planks would. The panels consisted of thinner boards, with their edges chamfered on one side so that the thin edges would fit into grooves in the stiles and rails. The panels were three sixteenths to a quarter of an inch thinner than the stiles. Therefore, as the panels were set flush with the frame on the front side, they left a recess or sink three sixteenths to a quarter of an inch deep on the back. The stiles and rails had a quarter-round molding formed on their inner edges to hold the panels in place. Not till much later was this molding made as a separate piece.

The first paneled doors had either two or three panels, but as time went on the number of panels was increased to four, five, and finally six. This does not mean that all later houses had six-paneled doors. The number of panels seems to have been a matter of preference on the part of the carpenter or owner, though the six-paneled types are more often found in the central-hall type of house, and those with two, three, four, or five panels are commoner in the central-chimney type. In a great many Early American houses as they exist today you will find both the batten and panel doors. The panel doors, in such cases, will generally be found on the most important rooms, and the batten type used for kitchen and back bedchambers.

For outside doors a combination of the sheathed and paneled types was used. This was actually a paneled door with a board lining. There were usually four panels on the earliest types, and the lining could be either horizontal or diagonal. While this was known as a sheathed or sheathing door, the same name was sometimes applied to the lined door when it was bound around with stiles and rails which formed a frame for it.

Toward the end of the eighteenth century both inside and outside doors were made with flat panels that were flush on one side and sunken on the other. On the flush side the panels had plain beading on the long edges. On the recessed side they were held in position by a simple, narrow molding.

One of the most interesting of external doors is the beveled-panel type, in which the front face of the panel is raised above the level of the stiles and rails. Even if the center part of the panel is flush with the surrounding woodwork, the result is very effective. You can readily tell the difference between the very old doors of this type and the more recent ones. The old doors will have the molding formed in one piece with the stiles and the rails. In those of newer construction the molding will be a separate piece applied after the panel was installed. There is one rare exception to this that we know of, in a house built before 1700. In this case the molding is more elaborate than the quarter-round and is applied separately. Insofar as the quarter-round molding is concerned, therefore, the rule holds good.

One kind of raised panel that is frequently encountered has the front surface of the panel sloping up toward the center. This forms what might be called a flat pyramid. Any panel of this type immediately labels the door as comparatively modern.

In none of these paneled doors are nails used; the joints are held together by small hardwood pegs.

The doors used to ward off evil spirits and their earthly counterparts were of two kinds—witch doors and Christian doors. Both of these utilize the sign of the cross to scare away all manner of evil things. The witch doors were used both on the outside and inside. Christian doors are found exclusively in interiors and may consist of one or two leaves. The single door is made with two small panels above two larger ones so that the center stile and rails form a vertical cross. In the double type the unfolding of the door or the joining of the two halves produces a similar result.

Witch doors also were of two types, one with the lower part of the door formed of four triangles so that the dividing rails formed an ✕ (or St. Andrew's cross). In the other type the two lower panels of a two-leaved door come together to form a cross whose arms curve down to the lower outer corners.

A type of witch door.

In some of the central-chimney type of houses the porch was so shallow between the front wall and the bottom of the stairs that there was not room for a wide door to swing fully open. This led the ingenious carpenters to split the door down the middle, forming a double or two-leaved door. These two halves were hinged to the two doorjambs so that they met in the center. Such double doors were used with even larger entries in order to permit large and bulky objects to be carried into the house. You will come across numbers of these today, both of the paneled and lined types.

During the early seventeenth century the Dutch introduced the door split horizontally across the middle, which, as a consequence, came to be called a Dutch door. The idea behind this type of door was that the top half could be opened to let in fresh air, while the bottom part remained closed to keep out animals and urchins. The earliest of these doors were formed of wide, vertical boards lined with a tenoned

An early doorway with simple transom.

frame made of wide and thick boards. This frame was open in the center. In New York State there are many examples of such construction with a bull's-eye light let into the outer boards of the upper section.

Other Dutch doors were made in the same manner as the lined doors, and sheathed ones with a double panel on the outside, top and bottom, were common. Other panel arrangements were four over two, four over four, and six over two. In all of these doors the shapes of the moldings used in the panels and across the top of the lower section are an excellent guide to their authenticity and age.

Another door that is often mentioned but rarely described is the funeral door. This is most commonly found on the wooden houses of the central-chimney type, though we have seen them on end-chimney houses, where they were not really needed. The door generally opens into the kitchen or keeping room from the outside, though sometimes it is found in the other front room. The purpose of this door is to permit the entry and egress of large furniture which the narrow front porch will not do. This was particularly important in the event of a funeral, when a long coffin could not be carried out in a dignified manner through the front door. Using the back door, if any, was of course out of the question. Since many of the funeral doors were hardly ever opened for any other purpose, it is only natural that they should acquire their name from their chief function.

On some of the smaller Early American-type houses the doorway trim was for a long time nothing more than a plain board frame. Sometimes the stiles and lintel were all of the same width. In other cases the lintel board was made wider (but not longer) to improve the balance. On others the doorways were made higher and more important-looking by the addition of a simple fanlight or transom. The practical purpose of the transoms was to let light into the tiny porch, which was often shut off from both rooms and stairs by doors. These transoms consisted of four, five, or six small panes extending across the top of the door. These are found on houses dating back to 1700 or earlier.

Over some of these lights a strip of wood extended out to protect them from the weather. This was soon followed by another plain board above the lights, with the flat strip placed on top of it, and usually made heavier and wider so that it projected farther out. This arrangement actually formed a simple architrave. To stop the doorway from looking topheavy, the boards forming the side trim were made wider and carried up to the architrave.

By the middle of the eighteenth century graduated moldings or consoles were added to support the projecting top piece, which by now formed a small cornice. The side trim was made more important by the addition of another flat board, somewhat narrower, on top of it. These narrow vertical pieces represented pilasters and were often molded or fluted on the front surface.

On the Georgian houses the whole door surround was made much more elaborate. Instead of the square lights and a simple architrave,

A simple architrave with pilasters makes a small doorway more imposing.

the doorway was crowned with a pediment, complete with frieze and cornice. After 1750 these doorways were capped with a true fanlight —fan-shaped or semicircular. On two houses that we know of the fanlight was represented by moldings tacked onto the flat surface, and there was no glass at all.

Still later—after the Revolution—some of these small Georgians acquired tiny entrance porches composed of two or three low steps, on top of which small columns upheld the pediment over an elliptical fanlight. Sidelights served to brighten the hall inside and give the doorway an even more massive and important look.

Restoration of doors often resolves itself into taking out the existing doors and replacing them with authentic types of the approximate age of the house. This, naturally, involves a great deal of work; it means hunting down old doors somewhere near the size you need. If all or most of the doors have been replaced by Victorian or even more modern atrocities, the job may prove almost impossible without the expenditure of much time and effort. On the other hand we know from practical experience that the demand for old doors is far less than the amount of restoration work in progress would suggest.

When wreckers and old-house specialists failed, we have found small builders and jobbing carpenters who have salvaged old doors and placed so low a valuation on them that they have been left in the open to rot. In one case we drove fifty miles to see what a small contractor might have in the way of old pine. He had none, but we did find the doors we needed. From one of them he had taken the original latch and sold it for twenty-five dollars. The door, a sheathed type about 150 years old and complete with thirty-inch hinges, we got for three dollars.

Doors can be found, but it is as well not to expect one that needs only to be hung. The size is rarely exact, and practically always the doorways are out of plumb. Where a door of the required type cannot be found, one may possibly be made up from old paneling lined with equally old sheathing. Some salvage specialists make a practice of such work.

If an old batten door is required, the thing to look for is the hand-made nails, provided the house was built before 1795, or if it was built later but has such nails in other parts of its construction. Such a door can be rebuilt, if necessary, by carefully straightening out the nail clinches and removing the nails. The boards and battens can then be trimmed to size and reassembled with the original nails. If the door has been used in a dry place, the nails will be in good condition, and most of them can be taken out without breaking off more than half an inch of the points.

Some old batten doors, made before 1800 or slightly after, may be fastened together with screws. If this is so, the screws will be of the handmade variety, with square ends. Often, however, the batten door can be cut down without taking it apart. If it needs to be made half an inch or so larger, strips of old wood can be glued and nailed to the ends or sides. If the wood is as old as the rest of the door, it will be easy to match the color, and the joint can be made practically unnoticeable so far as the vertical boards are concerned. The top and bottom strips, which should be put on last, and held between extensions of the side strips, may be notched to represent the board joints or beads. If the door is to be painted, the matching of the wood is not important, but the added wood should be thoroughly dried and seasoned so that it will not warp and shrink. If it does shrink and expand with the changing seasons, it will then be at the same rate as the door and no crack will appear. The glue should be one of the modern waterproof glues, and the strip clamped tightly until the glue is set hard. If the strip is applied slightly thicker than the door, after the glue is set it can be sanded down level. It is better to use thin wood dowels to attach the strips, rather than finishing nails.

Cutting down one of the sheathed doors is a much more difficult job because the stiles and rails of the outside, paneled portion must not be made too skimpy. On original doors these frame members are rarely less than four inches wide, and the bottom rail is usually half as deep again. Probably half an inch of the top rail and the stiles will be hidden by the rabbet of the door lintel and jambs when the door is closed, and we have to keep this in mind in trimming them down.

If such a door has not been previously cut, it is sometimes possible to take off half to three quarters of an inch all around without ruining the appearance of the door. This, of course, is a job for a power saw; it should never be attempted by hand. And all nails near the edges should be removed first.

When a house settles, doorframes become distorted by one jamb dropping below the level of the other. The peculiar result of this is that the doorframe is pulled out of shape, but the two sides remain parallel to one another, as do the top and bottom. As a consequence, if you fit a door to this opening you will have to trim off a triangular piece from the top and put it on the bottom. And since the two jambs will be closer together, you will also have to take a straight strip off the width of the door.

Before attempting any of this, it will pay to examine the doorframe to see if it cannot be squared, at least a little. Sometimes the low jamb can be raised slightly by wedging. This will tend to make the opening wider and push the jamb tight against the wall. It will also probably lift the door bottom up from the sill and necessitate packing one end of the threshold board to suit.

An important point to watch in fitting doors that are out of square is the floor clearance. If the door is hinged on the high side, it may hit the floor when it is opened. If it is hung on the low side, the clearance between the bottom of the door and the floor will increase as the door opens wider. Switching the hinges from one side to the other may solve the problem in some instances. In other cases trickery may have to be resorted to. If the hinges are of the butt type, new hinges which cause the door to rise slightly as it opens can be substituted. These are called rising hinges. The same effect can be secured with specially made flap hinges of various kinds, or even bar hinges or half-straps. The rise usually need not be much if a fairly thick threshold or saddle is used.

Sagging doors are another problem entirely. The sag usually comes from shrinkage which loosens boards and panels and frames. Pegs also may be broken or parts of the wood rotted. In most instances the doors can be squared by applying pressure to the diagonally opposite corners (the low one and the high one), after the door has been taken off the hinges. The means of keeping it square after this operation depend upon the type of door and the cause of the trouble. On frame doors HL hinges are a big help, and on exterior doors L-shaped antique pintle-strap hinges are generally effective.

For the first part of the job the best tool is a long cramp composed of one fixed and one sliding jaw mounted on a length of three-quarter-inch pipe. These cramp jaws, one of which incorporates a screw device for tightening, can be bought very cheaply at almost any hardware store.

If the door is of the batten type, the best remedy is to take off the battens and fasten them tightly on again after squaring the upright boards. If necessary, a third or fourth batten can be added. For doors on outbuildings a diagonal batten may be used, extending from the hinge side at the bottom to the outer edge at the top. If there is a central batten, the diagonal can be installed in two sections.

For paneled doors it may be necessary to drive thin wedges alongside the tenon tongues in the mortise holes. The wedges should first be dipped in glue. Failing this, it is a simple matter to knock out the pins from the joints and take the door to pieces. It can then be re-assembled, the joints glued and cramped together. It is then repinned with wood pegs or dowels while in the cramps. At the same time any cracked panels can be glued and spacing strips put in the grooves in the stiles and rails to take up the panel shrinkage.

Before undertaking a job of this kind it is as well to survey the whole situation. In a very old house out-of-square doors are to be expected, and so long as they work and show no large gaps between the head and lintel or foot and floor, they can very well be left alone. On the other hand, if there are gaps and the frame is badly out of square, the door may be made to fit by adding wedge-shaped strips top and bottom.

Double doors introduce problems of their own, especially on wooden houses. In many cases where a single door has been substituted for a double door, the doorframe has been narrowed. On many houses the double doors were made four feet wide so that opening one leaf would permit an ordinary-sized person to enter. If they have been narrowed, the whole doorway will probably have been altered too. Widening it again will then involve considerable work, especially if there is a transom. It is therefore best to leave the doorway alone unless it is necessary to restore it architecturally. If the inside porch is so narrow that it interferes with the opening of the wide door, double ones of the same width can be substituted. Such doors, however, are much harder to find than single doors, and it may be necessary to make a pair from a single door or from a pair of suitable panels.

We have done this very successfully by sawing an old lined door in two from top to bottom. This, of course, makes the center rail very narrow, but this is compensated for by adding a strip to each side and rabbeting them to form the center joint or meeting bars of the door.

An extension that has grown; lean-to additions front and rear forming a monitor roof. An expert would have difficulty identifying the type of original dwelling.

A Southern early eighteenth-century house with all fireplaces at one end. Dormers and porch apparently original. Note upper parts of chimneys spaced away from gable. (*Courtesy The New-York Historical Society, New York.*)

A one-and-a-half story New England Colonial house of 1775 with twentieth-century porch and large window lights.

The same house as above, partially restored. The original fanlight remains to be replaced together with a lower door. All upstairs windows in gables and rear.

# Doors and Doorways

The door was made, in this instance, to fit the narrow opening by shaving down the width of the stiles on both sides. In order to keep the narrow doors stiff and prevent them from bowing inward, three hinges were used on each leaf. The job of hanging such doors, we found, is much simplified if screw-type gudgeons are used. The pins then can be lined up by simply screwing them a little farther in or out as required. Regulating the spike type is much more difficult, and they are more likely to pull loose with use. It has, we are constantly being reminded, always been difficult to make doors fit well when they are hung on pintle-strap hinges or half-straps. The reason, it seems, is that the fit between the hinge eye and the gudgeon pin is always too loose. The remedy is to have gudgeons made that will fit well, and to see that the hinge eyes are not too worn. If the eyes are badly worn they can be strengthened and made perfectly circular by pressing either an iron collar or a brass bushing into them. If iron is used, the collar can be welded to the hinge so as to make a solid unit.

Putting old doors back into their original condition very often begins with replacing the hardware with authentic specimens of the same date as the doors. What these should consist of is discussed fully elsewhere. The major problem is likely to be what to do with the holes and marks left by the latches and hinges that are removed. The most serious scars are likely to be left by holes cut for the latch lift.

The common practice of plugging these holes with plastic wood is not to be recommended. A much better procedure is to cut the hole square with a sharp mortise chisel and plug it with a piece of old wood of a similar grain. The hole and plug can be tapered slightly and the plug glued before being pressed in. A light sanding when the glue is dry will remove irregularities and make a patch almost invisible. Any new hole that is made should be as small as will serve the purpose, though the edges may be sanded with smooth paper to simulate wear.

# CHAPTER X

# Fixing the Floors

IN THE days when large oak and pine trees were plentiful, stout boards from twelve to twenty inches wide and suitable for flooring were obtainable throughout most of the colonies. The practice of using these wide boards lasted until the beginning of the nineteenth century in places where they were still available, such as the western states. In places like Ohio, where the hard pine was scarcer, ash very often took its place. In these areas we have also encountered floors of chestnut and even yellow poplar!

In the earliest Colonial houses, oak predominated, and although it continued to be used till 1800 or later, white pine replaced it in the northern colonies and the harder yellow pine in the southern ones. Whichever wood was used, the manner of applying it to floors remained approximately the same. The boards were rarely less than an inch thick, and some were as much as an inch and a half thick.

The two general methods of closing the joints between the boards were either to form them with half-lap joints or to cover the joint underneath with a thinner board. It is quite common to find both systems used in the same house. Less common, no doubt because of the expense, was the loose-tongue joint. You will find this more often in the later and better-built houses, particularly if the floors are of pine or chestnut. To make this joint, the edges of both boards were grooved and a separate, thin piece of wood inserted in the grooves. This made a much more even floor than the half-lap joint because both boards were prevented from moving either up or down in relation to each other. In all cases that we have seen, most of the floor boards were long enough to extend the full width of the floor, or at least from one principal beam to another.

Some houses of 1700 have the floor boards fastened to the joists with pegs, but by that time the use of nails was becoming common. Normal practice then was—up to the end of the eighteenth century—

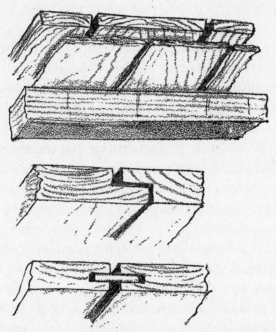

Three methods of laying old-time floor
boards.

to use boards of random widths. But in later houses the boards may be more evenly matched. In either case the boards will be nailed to each joist, with two nails to each narrow board and three nails to the wide ones. Up to 1795, and sometimes later, these were the large, hand-made nails, and no attempt was made to hide them. Since the overlaps and the tongues were at least half an inch wide, there was room for some shrinkage without leaving a space or crack through the floor. On the other hand there might be a considerable gap between the two edges of the joint, which is an untidy feature from our modern viewpoint.

[ 131 ]

The boards which did not have halved or tongue joints had the gaps between them sealed by thin boards underneath them. The under boards were rough-sawn, thin boards, that the old-timers called "slit-work," half to three eighths of an inch thick. Their edges generally were not trimmed. These boards were laid on the joists, with an occasional nail to hold them in position while the finish boards were laid over them. In some cases the under boards were quite narrow and extended only two or three inches on either side of the joint between the boards above them. In other instances the under boards practically touched one another and formed what was really a double floor.

After a century or more of use, many of these floors became uneven, owing to wear or warping, or breaking of the nails. The wide joints were often unsatisfactory to meticulous housekeepers and spoiled linoleum that was laid over them. Consequently we find that many such floors have been removed, or replaced with six-inch tongue-and-groove pine, or narrower hardwood, or such floors have been laid over them. Usually, removing an old oak floor is not easy. The wood is brittle with age, and the nails, perfectly preserved, refuse to budge. The result is broken or damaged boards that have little salvage value. That is one reason why it is difficult to buy used oak floor boards. Pine boards do not present the same problem because, with or without clipping the nailheads off, they are more easily removed. Generally smaller nails were used to hold the pine because they could be driven into the soft wood without bending.

Some of the problems facing the new old-house owner, then, are what to do with wide joints, warped and squeaky boards, worn or damaged surfaces, and floors that need restoration of some kind. To take the worst case first, your floors may have been entirely uncared for. If the boards are of oak (in the South they may be of long-leaf pine that looks much like it!) they will ordinarily show less wear and more evidences of damage than almost any other flooring. The first thing to do is to take out the warps as much as possible. A preliminary to this is to see that they are properly fastened down. If nails have pulled out, or the boards are badly warped in a crosswise direction, this should be corrected as far as possible before grinding away any wood with a sander. Loose nails and those that project above the surface should be driven in solidly and set below the surface of the wood, using a nail set or punch, to allow for sanding. Extra nails should be used to pull down warped sections. These nails should be of the same type as those already in the floor—either old handmade ones or the early type of machine-cut nails. Sources from which these can be obtained are discussed under that subject head. If modern nails must be used, heavy-gauge finishing nails will serve, and they can be driven in at an angle between the boards where they will not be seen.

If the board has been bent upward by warping so that the high part is unduly worn, nailing it down against the joist will pull it below the general level. This can be avoided by packing the board up from underneath by pushing or driving a piece of shingle between the joist and the board. The floor board can then be nailed firmly at that point. This same procedure is sometimes used in the case of squeaking boards. Squeaking is caused by the movement of the board and can be checked by bedding the board solidly, either through packing or nailing.

If the space between the board and the joist has been caused by the joist sagging, the remedy is obvious—support the joist with a post! In the case of upstairs floors, of course, this is impossible, and you may have to take up the board to insert packing. If this will not do the trick, the joist may have to be stiffened by having boards nailed to its sides, or it may even have to be replaced. Fortunately such a condition rarely arises.

Sagging floors are not particularly common, except in cases where a house is so far gone that its floors have been rained on and rotted. In any case the sag is usually the result of a warping of either the joists or the beams. In more serious cases the cause is the rotting of the wood or the settling or tilting of part of the foundation. Such sagging must not be confused with the slanting of floors, which is another problem altogether. By far the most common cause of sagging, then, is the bending of one or perhaps two joists, or even the collapse of a joist. In most instances the trouble occurs in connection with the ground floor and the sag can be corrected by jacking up the part of the joist involved and inserting a post to support it at that point. If there already is a post, the height can be increased by inserting wedges between the post top and the joist. It is simpler to insert these while the joist is being held up by a jack, but if they are flat enough they may be driven in. Professional repairers often have two men to drive in the wedges, one on each side, both striking simultaneously. In jacking up the joist, take care not to lift it too far. We have seen ceilings ruined and wall plaster cracked by too much enthusiasm in this operation.

If it is an upstairs floor that sags, the cure may have to be more drastic—the replacement of a joist or the insertion of a beam right across the room to support them all. Such a beam would, of course, have to be held either by masonry (a chimney or gable) or by posts.

With all of these things taken care of, you can proceed with your sanding, but don't overdo it! Floors that have been sanded until they are perfectly flat and smooth might just as well be new. They have no character, and contrast too sharply with the rest of the woodwork, so that they spoil the feel of the whole room.

If you are installing a heating system in the house for the first time, you may expect to find that the boards—and indeed all the woodwork —will shrink. If no humidifier is incorporated in the heating plant— an unthinkable omission in these progressive times—the shrinkage may be serious. Usually, open joints up to a quarter inch wide can be filled with some special crack-filling compound. If the space is too wide for this treatment to be effective, the only lasting remedy is to relay the boards, clamping them tightly together before nailing. Since this will most likely necessitate the insertion of a narrow strip of flooring to take up the extra space, you should start at a fireplace wall and work toward an outside wall. This will enable you to put the new wood near a wall where it will be least obvious.

In the filling of joint cracks you have first to be sure that the crack does not extend right through to the underside of the boards—as it will if there is no sealed joint or if the lap is insufficient. The first step then is to close the joint from underneath so that the filler will not fall through. This can be done by tacking strips of lathing or thin board on the underside or by using some insulating board to fill the space between the joists and so accomplishing two useful purposes at once. If this is not practical, as in the case of upstairs rooms with a ceiling

Sealing floor joints to retain crack filler.

underneath, you will have a difficult problem on your hands. The simplest method of forming a bed for the filler is then to insert wooden strips into the cracks. These strips should be of some stiff wood, made as wide as the crack will permit, and an eighth or three sixteenths of an inch thick. They need only be long enough to reach the centers of the two adjacent joists. If there is already a half joint, this will keep the strip from falling through. If necessary you can glue the strips before inserting them.

Undoubtedly the best crack filler for old floors is the plastic-wood type. If it is of the proper consistency it is possible to fill the crack without the use of a wood retaining strip, but the strip simplifies the operation tremendously.

In all cases it is necessary to stain the filler to match the color of the floor boards. This can be done either before or after filling the crack. A dry color can be used for this purpose, obtainable in powder form. To get an even color throughout, the powder is best mixed with the filler first. Rubbing the powder into the filled crack is a messy job and does not produce really satisfactory results. If the crack has been filled with the raw filler, the only thing to do is to stain it with a ready-made stain, such as one of the Minwax series, after it has dried and set and been sanded down smooth and level. After staining, the filler can be lightly rubbed over with steel wool. The dry colors oftenest used are raw sienna, yellow ocher, and raw umber. To match old oak you use mostly raw sienna. If this is not yellow enough, you can add yellow ocher. If it is too light, a dash of raw umber (not the burnt) will darken it. For old pine, raw sienna and ocher will probably be required, always remembering that it is better to have the cracks darker than the wood rather than lighter.

Plastic wood is the trade name for the filler made with a plastic solvent. There is another form, that you have to mix with water, called wood putty. We have had good results with both of them, but the putty is considerably the cheaper. The mineral-type crack filler is not suitable for old floors. The floors always have enough spring in them to dislodge it after a while, and, being composed of plaster, it rapidly cracks and disintegrates.

It is a disagreeable fact that floors which shrink during the winter when the furnace heat is on will probably expand again in the warmer weather. This seasonal widening and closing of the floor joints makes it practically impossible for the crack filler to remain in good condition throughout the year. If it is installed in the summer it will be loose in the winter. If it is put in during the cold weather it will be squeezed in the warm and may cause warping of the boards. But until some filler is devised that will contract when the boards expand, and vice versa, we shall have to take our chances on that. The results need not be serious, and a narrow crack between the floor boards is something the old-house owner can well afford to countenance without too much loss of sleep.

In filling deep scars and nailhead holes in floor boards, much greater care should be taken to match the color exactly. This is very easy to do when you are working with the small quantities usually involved in disguising damage to the boards. But here, as in all treatments of the floors, as little should be done as possible to renew the surface. The old boards almost always have a patina that cannot be replaced once it is destroyed except by time, and so long as holes and cracks and scars do not interfere with their use, they should be preserved as records of long and honorable service.

# Fixing the Floors

Usually there will not be a great many nail holes to fill, unless another floor has been laid over the old one. This happens quite often, especially in towns, where hardwood floors, not so long ago, were a hallmark of gentility. Fortunately for the restorer, in the majority of instances the new boards were not nailed directly to the old ones. The general practice was to nail wood furring strips to the floor and fasten the new floor to them. The furring usually consists of strips of wood about an inch and a half thick and two inches high. Under them would probably be building paper covering the whole floor as a dust excluder. The strips were generally toenailed to the old floor, but thin ones may have been nailed through. If they are toenailed from both sides, care has to be taken in removing them not to tear out slivers of the old floor. The best method is to pry up the strips gently with a chisel or other flat tool so as to lift the nails, then knock it down so that the nailheads will be left protruding above the surface. With a good claw hammer or a pair of pincers the nails can easily be yanked out.

In cases where the new boards are actually nailed to the old ones, equal care has to be taken in getting the nails out, particularly if blind nailing has been used. Blind nails are driven in from the sides of the boards so that they will not show when the adjoining boards are inserted. This is the same thing as toenailing, and removing the nails is troublesome.

Among the many desperate things that are done in the name of restoration is the use of good floor boards for other and quite foreign purposes. We have, on occasion, been invited to admire the beautiful old paneling in a keeping room, made from the floor boards of an attic. The living room looked uncomfortable in its new dress, which was quite out of keeping with its date and style, and the boards had been so worked over to disguise their origin that they looked painfully new. In happy contrast to this was the excellent salvage job another friend had done in using the floor of one room to repair three others. The house had been in particularly bad shape when he took it over. All of the upstairs floors had damaged or broken boards. Unable to match any of them, he had, in desperation, torn up the floor of the least-used room and taken the boards to patch up the others. Later he was able to acquire some fifty-year-old pine which made a presentable floor for the room he had robbed.

In still another case a passable job was made of a badly scarred pine floor by turning most of the boards over. Fortunately they were fairly smooth, and the delicate golden hue of age survived the application of oil and wax and steel wool.

## Refinishing Floors

Nothing contributes so much to the charm of an old-fashioned room as time-mellowed woodwork, and an old oak or pine floor can be a thing of beauty in itself. But since floors must be serviceable as well as interesting, the surface applied to them must be durable and easily maintained. In colonial days the early floors of small houses were left in their raw state, until the days when paints became common. And, in the course of years, the bare wood darkened as it acquired the scars and stains and evidences of wear that give it its character today. In the nineteenth century many of these floors were oiled or waxed, and later shellacked or varnished. The oils and waxes brought out the beauty of the grain and gave the wood a rich color. In the later eighteenth century other floors were painted, some to lose their paint by wear or deliberate removal, and the rest to be repainted periodically up to the present day. So interesting and old-fashioned-looking is bare wood considered to be that nine out of every ten old floors are stripped to the surface or deeper. And far too often they lose their mellow patina through too ardent application of the sanding machine.

Quite often we have been introduced to eighteenth-century floors with a spatter finish. Now spattered floors were not thought of before 1840, and possibly a few years after that, so they are not authentic in earlier houses. There are, however, a number of other paint finishes that were popular in pre-Revolutionary and post-Revolutionary days. In those years the floors of smaller houses were being decorated in the same manner as the larger ones had been from 1750 on. Traveling decorators, who journeyed through the countryside, en route from town to town, are thought to have been responsible for many of these works of art. Usually it was the best room of the house that had a painted floor, and the designs varied according to the skill of the painter and, doubtless, the taste of the owner and the price he was prepared to pay.

The earlier designs were painted freehand, but later on stenciling became the vogue. Occasionally the designs covered the whole floor, or the pattern may have been confined to borders, with or without solid color in the middle. Geometric designs were favorites in many sections, and the commonest background color was yellow ocher. Over this patterns were worked out in reds, blues, greens, and white. A later development was the painting of floors to look like marble.

If you are fortunate enough to have such a decorated floor, every effort should be made to restore the original pattern. If it has been painted over, this will call for long and painstaking effort and is really a job for an expert. If you can get no expert help, try gently washing a small area with a solvent such as denatured alcohol or turpentine. By this means you may be able to remove enough of the covering paint to allow you to copy off a full unit of the design. If the decoration is in bad condition, it probably will be worth while to restencil your floor, working from this pattern. But, whatever you do, be sure to let your local antiquarian society know it's there! They will certainly be interested enough to help you.

The finish that is given to any floor will depend not only upon the kind of wood, but also on the treatment it has received in the past, as well as its present condition. For most undecorated floors a generally satisfactory finish is an occasional oil rub, or oiling followed by waxing. This both darkens the wood and brings out the grain. Darkening strengthens the warmer tones that are so desirable, and the hard wax helps to preserve the surface and make it easier to clean. The modern treatment of applying shellac or varnish is not recommended. This puts on a thin, hard veneer which quickly wears through, and the worn areas show unmistakably for what they are. Such floors when waxed are inclined to be both glossy and slippery.

Of all the floor treatments we have tried, the oiling seems the best, if you do not want a glossy surface. Gloss looks out of place in an old-time room anyway! If you have been able to save the original surface of the wood by limiting sanding to a brief cleaning with fine sand-paper, the oil will give the boards a fairly even tone. But if there is wear, or sanding has cut through the old surface, it is best to use a mild stain finish and wax over that. If you get the proper kind of finish it will contain both the stain and the preservative materials. Unlike shellac, this finish will penetrate the fibers of the wood and make them the same color right through. Wear will then not be so obvious, because the color of the wood will not change. Regular waxing thereafter will maintain the soft finish luster without making the surface slippery.

# CHAPTER XI

# The Eyes of the House

AN ESSENTIAL feature of the Old Colonial, and one to which those houses owe much of their charm, is the small-paned window. From the inside, those windows give the rooms a cozy air and a protective feeling. Externally, they constitute one of the most important architectural features of the house. If you have ever seen an old Colonial house with windows composed of two large sheets of glass, you will understand vividly what is meant. Large areas of glass in a wall have the same effect as holes. The windows are nothing more than blank air spaces that give no support to the structure above. And, what is worse, they rob the house of that feeling of privacy which is, or should be, a fundamental characteristic of any dwelling that we call a home.

There are, of course, several other principles in connection with the windows that have to be kept in mind in restoring and remodeling. The size and placement of the windows in each wall, technically known as fenestration, affect the whole appearance and feeling of the house. The important thing in restoration is to install windows as close to the original in size and details of construction as possible. If there are some of the old windows left, the task is easy. If they have all been replaced by modern ones, a little investigation is called for. Fortunately we have a great deal more latitude in this respect than the early builders had. In the early 1700s glass was comparatively scarce and costly. As a result windows were small and panes tiny. During the eighteenth century these conditions changed entirely, and the majority of house owners put in larger windows, or at least bigger panes. The result was, generally but not always, an improvement in appearance. This periodic change in window styles, incidentally, offers us a useful indication of the age of the house, provided we can be certain that the house has its original windows.

The arrangement of the windows in the house tell us a number of things. Prior to 1700 most windows were placed at random and were tiny, giving the gable ends of some early houses an amusingly casual appearance. But by the beginning of the eighteenth century windows had settled into a system of two to each downstairs room, with five across the second floor if the house was a full two stories high. Most lean-to houses, however, continued, until about 1750, to make use of small windows spread at random over the gables. After 1750 some houses were built with a Palladian window on the second floor. As explained earlier, the Palladian window consists of a large window flanked by two smaller ones. The central window is not only higher than the others, but has a rounded top. It was used on the later Georgian, central-hall type of house and by 1800 had become very elaborate in detail. Properly the Palladian window was perched over the front door, but some carpenter-builders became so enamored of it that they duplicated it in the attic gables.

In some early-nineteenth-century houses, when houses as a whole were being less lavishly decorated, the top of the center window was lopped off so that all three were of the same height. This operation converted the Palladian into a plain triple window that was much used on Greek Revival houses. At this time other houses were built with six windows across the second-floor front.

As may be expected, there are exceptions to all these arrangements. For example, there are numbers of one-and-a-half-story Early Americans of the central-chimney type with no windows on the second-floor front at all. These will probably have two windows evenly spaced on each side of the front door, with the gables containing one window for each of the downstairs rooms, two for the front bedroom upstairs, and one for each rear bedroom.

# The Eyes of the House

On another type of one-and-a-half-story house, built after 1800, there may be two or more "eyebrow" windows under the front eaves. These ordinarily consist of a single row of two to four lights, but on some later houses they may be two rows high. Inside, these lie-on-your-stomach windows are only a few inches above the floor level. They are a possible solution of the ventilation problem in cases where dormers are not practical or permissible, but they should not be used on any other type of house.

The variety of gable windows on the third floor in Greek Revival houses built after 1800 is endless. The first windows were small, single, and extremely simple and rectangular. The window might be made up of two large panes surrounded by half a dozen narrow strips of glass, or some simple modification of that arrangement. These windows gradually became more ornate and pretentious, assuming every conceivable shape—diamond, fan, oval, triangular, and so on. Where the early ones had wooden muntins, these soon gave way to metal bars and leaded lights. Where there was no need for a window, imitation fanlights were sometimes painted on. In the more western states, where Greek Revival was pushed to its limits, frets took the place of windows, sometimes with glass behind them and sometimes without.

It is said that dormer windows appeared first in Virginia, in the middle of the seventeenth century. Whether this is so or not, there is no doubt that they have long been popular, especially in the South, and appear on almost every style of roof, except the gable roof of the Greek Revival house. A characteristic of the Southern Colonial dormer is its extreme height compared to its width. On small dwellings they are usually simple and devoid of ornamentation except, perhaps, for a small pediment. There are three general kinds of dormer windows: those set into the roof, those which project entirely beyond the slope of the roof, and the long, continuous dormer which disfigures almost any roof. Some of them are gabled and others flat, but this depends upon the style of architecture of the house and not the date.

*Sash and Frame Evolution*

The earliest type of window was the leaded casement, which lingered in some parts till 1715 or so. There may be a few odd windows of this kind still in existence on houses built since 1700, but they are extremely rare. In fact the chances of finding an old casement type of window, with leaded diamond-shaped panes, is extremely remote. The casement window is hinged at the side like a door. Sometimes two or more of these windows were grouped, with a small pillar or upright called a mullion dividing them. The tiny panes of glass were known as "quarries"—a term then applied to all window glass regardless of shape—and they were held in place by lead "calmes." Long after the double-sash window came in, casement windows were still used on the sides and rear of houses.

In the year 1715 the double-hung or guillotine window made its appearance in the homes of the well-to-do. The sashes were usually, but not always, four panes wide and three panes high—twelve lights in all to each sash. This formed what is known as a twelve-over-twelve window. When larger-sized glass was used some windows were made three lights wide, making the window a nine-over-nine. Common practice was to fix the top sash so that it would not move and to arrange the lower one so that it could be lifted part way for ventilation. Since there was no means of counterbalancing the sash, it was rather heavy to lift. This is what may have led to the adoption of windows which had more lights in the top than the bottom sash, though there are windows in which this arrangement is reversed. The lighter bottom sash then had one row of panes less than the upper one, making it a twelve-over-nine, or a nine-over-six, or perhaps a twelve-over-eight. Another reason sometimes given for this practice is that with both halves of the window the same size the wide sash-frame members (the meeting bars) are at eye level. This would be better logic if everyone were of the same height and all windows the same size. Although oak was used in the early days for the frames, the later ones were made of pine

An original doorway to a Nantucket town house of 1731. The handrails, typical of the early 1800s, were added in 1890. (*Courtesy Mrs. E. F. May.*)

A Dutch entrance of the very late eighteenth century, the Dutch "kick" of the roof being supported by wooden pillars. Dutch door and settles go together. (*Courtesy The New-York Historical Society, New York.*)

A Connecticut doorway of 1752 with built-up stone steps and an unusual halved door with lights. The narrow clapboard is of interest. (*Courtesy The New-York Historical Society, New York.*)

Dutch door with bull's-eye lights in raised panels and original knocker latch. Moulding between door halves is missing. Lion's head knocker is later. (*Courtesy The New-York Historical Society, New York.*)

This shows how a kitchen and woodshed extension can be made an architectural unit with the house by repetitions of the eyebrow windows and frieze. The eighteenth-century house was remodeled in 1815 in the fashionable Greek Revival style. (*Courtesy Robert S. Carraway, Esq.*)

A simple eighteenth-century town house of brick in Delaware, with decorative slate roof. Lower sashes are modern substitutes. Small door at left is servants' entrance. (*Courtesy The New-York Historical Society, New York.*)

because of the ease with which it could be worked and its better weathering qualities.

The most obvious characteristics of a very early window are the heaviness of the muntins and the fact that the glass is almost flush with them in the front. This gives the whole window a flat appearance and makes the panes look even smaller than they are. The sashes of these old windows had very thin and narrow rails. The use of thin rails was

An early-type window showing
method of retaining glass.

made necessary by the thinness of the walls, which often did not exceed four inches, especially if they were of the plank-frame type.

The early frames were set flush with the inside wall and projected well beyond the outside surface. Another earmark of the period was the fact that the window heads and sills were wide enough to extend beyond the jambs (the vertical side members), where they were framed into the studs. In this period it became fashionable to mold the sills. This was the only way in which the window was decorated.

In later houses, built during the last quarter of the eighteenth century, the muntins were made much thinner. The head and sill were flush with the jambs, and the interior trim, consisting of five-eighths-

or three-quarter-inch boards, set on top of the plaster. This, combined
with the extra thickness of the walls, brought the frame farther back
into the wall. The frame was next covered with a casing on the outside, and this was often decorated with moldings all around, or ornamentation of the top corners. In most parts this development took
place between 1760 and 1800.

By the end of the century many a window had advanced from a
simple projecting weatherboard above the head to a full-blown archi-

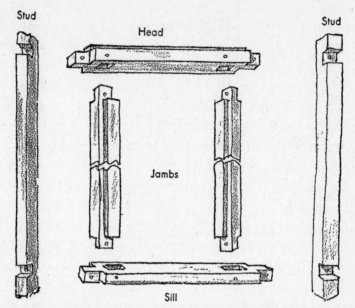

Structural members of an early-type window frame.

trave or pediment. Such adornments, including a casing, were even
added to earlier windows. In houses of stone and brick, similar decorative features are found, sometimes in contrasting stone or brick, or
even wood.

These old windows are much simpler in construction than the modern ones which have cords and counterweights. It is a curious fact that
a sash-balancing system was advertised as early as 1757, but there
seems to be no record of any such thing ever being used, at least on the
smaller houses. In the earlier houses the window frame consists of two

vertical members, usually four inches thick, which form the jambs; a head which connects them at the top, and the sill into which the jambs are framed. Both head and sill were made long enough to frame into the studs. In later structures, where the windows were wider, two studs often formed the jambs, with pieces of wood the same size nailed or framed into them to form the sill support and the head. The jambs and head were boxed in with plain boards, and a similar trim surrounded the window on the inside. If the inside of the window bottom was covered with paneling, such as a dado or wainscot, the capping would take the place of the bottom trim. In other cases a flat board formed an inside sill against which the back of the lower sash rested. The outside sill would be a broad, heavy piece of wood, usually oak, with the top beveled so as to drain off water. This would extend under the jamb casing as far as the stud.

The trim and sashes were both made of pine in place of the earlier oak. The rabbet for the sash was made from a separate piece of wood, wide at the bottom and cut back at the top to form a step on which the top sash rested. The lower sash fitted against the wide part and was held in position by a strip of molding nailed to the jamb. The top of the upper sash was kept from moving by a flat strip nailed to the underside of the head. There was no parting bead, as there is in modern windows, to separate the two sashes. The two meeting rails, in later windows, were sometimes cut at an angle so that, with the lower sash down, the rails would wedge against one another and make a tight joint.

In many of the later windows the top sash was allowed to move up and down three or four inches, by cutting the step lower. It was held in its uppermost position by means of one or a pair of spring catches mounted in the sash side rails and fitting into holes in the jamb. Another type of catch often used was mounted in the jamb and fitted into notches cut in the edge of the sash. The bottom sash also had the same kind of catch which enabled it to be opened to various heights.

# Old American Houses

*Old Glass and New*

One deciding factor in the size of old windows was the size of the glass pane available. In the early days the panes were all small. The smallest we find mention of were 4 × 6 inches, and for a long time one of the most popular sizes was 6 × 8 inches. Numerous attempts were made to manufacture window glass in the colonies, but without much success. Up to 1750 or so most of the glass was imported from England, and not until after 1783 did the domestic manufacture of glass begin to boom. The sizes of glass panes advertised by dealers at that time included 4 × 6 inches, 4 × 8, 4 × 9, 5 × 7, 6 × 8, 7 × 9, 8 × 10, 8 × 12½, 9 × 11, 9 × 12, 10 × 12, 11 × 13, and 12 × 14.

The early glass, however, was far from satisfactory, judged by present-day standards. It was iridescent, owing to impurities, it had streaks and bubbles and a wavy surface, so that looking through it was a sad strain on the eyes. It did, however, let in a good deal of light, and that after all was its main function. Today it is the defects of the old glass that make it interesting.

The oldest, and crudest, of the glass panes were very thin and uneven. The color was a greenish gray, with iridescent patches, and to the touch it felt more like a piece of earthenware biscuit than what it was. You may still encounter odd pieces of it in back windows, cellars, or fanlights. Later glass was much clearer and whiter, sometimes with a slight amethyst hue. Such panes add considerable interest to the windows they adorn.

The small sizes of these early panes was due to the way in which they were made. In the earliest process the glass was first blown into a large thin sphere, like a giant bubble. A stick, called a pontil, was attached to the red-hot glass at the opposite side from the blowpipe. The blowpipe was then detached, leaving a two-inch hole in the sphere. The glass was put back into the furnace and, as it softened, the operator twirled the pontil. The softer the glass became, the faster it was whirled, and as it whirled, it expanded. Finally, with a loud pop, it burst open into a flat, circular sheet.

This sheet of glass, four feet in diameter, was gradually withdrawn from the furnace to cool. The operator now had a four-foot glass disk, uniformly thin except for the heavy blob where it was stuck to the pontil. When this was broken off, the thick part formed what was known as a bullion, or, more popularly, as a bull's-eye. The rest of the disk was cut into squares. The bull's-eye could readily be sold for use in door panels, for transoms, or for door sidelights. A great many of these bull's-eyes are found even today, set originally in the upper panels of Dutch doors throughout the Hudson Valley in New York. Today bull's-eyes a hundred and fifty years old fetch as much as fifteen dollars apiece!

Astonishing as it may seem, this process of making window glass continued to be used till well into the nineteenth century, when a somewhat similar but improved process was developed. Large-sized panes were made possible by the new method in which the glass was alternately blown and swung until it formed a long cylinder. These cylinders were up to twenty inches in diameter and almost six feet long. The cylinders were cut along one side and the glass flattened out to make sheets about five feet by six. But the sheet could never be properly flattened by hand, and the glass made by this method is generally slightly bowed and distorted.

### Doorway Lights

As security from hostile Indians and other unwelcome visitors became less of a problem to the colonists, they were able to pay more attention to getting light into their small entries and deep hallways. The first step in this direction was the installation of lights above the front door. The first and simplest arrangement, current in 1700, was a single row of five to eight panes across the width of the door. These were held in broad muntins, separated from the top of the door by a transom bar. The ends were enclosed by the doorway frame.

As in the case of the windows, the transom lights were set flush into the muntins, leaving very little space for putty. In later transoms the muntins were thinner and the glass set in deeper. By 1723 doors began to appear with similar lights set into them at the top, but this practice was never common. What it did do was to permit the use of a taller door in the same-sized door frame, without cutting down the amount of glass area.

After the Revolution both fanlights and sidelights were introduced in Georgian and Greek Revival houses. The fanlight which appeared

Decorative leaded fanlight, after 1800.

first was a semicircular or fan-shaped form of transom. It got its name from its shape and the radiating muntins. In the first of these fanlights wooden muntins were used. These were replaced, after 1800, by lead. Sometimes iron bars supported the glass at the back, and decorative lead strips formed a pattern on the front of the glass. Later types of fanlights were semi-elliptical and extremely ornate.

On the Early American houses 1760 saw the introduction of transom lights with arched tops and the use of such lights in the upper parts of the doors. This design of lights was much used in double (two-leaved) doors, especially when the design of the doorway allowed no room for a transom.

The first sidelights were narrow and similar in construction to the transoms. Later they became wider and followed the same trend of evolution as the fanlight, from straight wood muntins to fancy designs in lead. In some instances, where there was a really broad hall or entry to be lighted, the sidelights were made very wide, and even had sliding sashes.

## Window Trouble

Unless an old house has constantly been lived in and kept in good condition, one of the first places where deterioration will evidence itself is around the windows. Trouble may develop either in the frame or the sashes themselves. The chief causes will be the rain leaking in, which will rot or warp the wood; a settling of the old house which will throw the frames out of square; or some other faulty condition which will cause the windows to stick. Insects of various kinds have also been known to make trouble—wasps, carpenter ants, or termites, who make themselves at home in the woodwork and dig holes that let in the weather even if they do not chew the wood itself to pieces.

Any suspicious holes or sprinklings of powdered wood, or the sight of insects coming and going, should be investigated. It may be necessary to take the sashes out of the frame and remove any doubtful section of the woodwork. If the casing must come off, this usually is better done from the outside so as not to disturb the wall plaster. The sashes can easily be removed by taking out the small molding strip that runs up both sides of the frame—as a rule—and forms a guide for the lower sash. In some old houses only one side of the window has a detachable strip, the other side having the bead formed on the edge of the casing. This discovery once caused us considerable embarrassment and a badly marred window frame, so first make sure there is a joint between the bead and the board!

The underside of the sill also should be examined for signs of rot. This is one spot that collects water and is very often missed in painting. If the sashes are loose in the frame, the casing can be removed from one jamb and packed out with strips of old shingle, then replaced. In cases where the window is out of square, the sashes may be made to fit top and bottom by trimming off one and adding to the other as in the case of doors. The important fact to watch here is that any such carving does not move the meeting bars out of line with one another. If the movement of the frame has tightened the jambs against the sashes so that they are hard to move, the remedy is to plane or sand the side rails of the sashes. Afterwards the raw wood should be given a coat of paint primer, thin varnish, or heavy lemon oil to keep out the damp.

Broken spring catches are easily replaced. The tubular-bolt type can be forced out of the sash while you have it out of the frame. The other type that fits in the jamb is also removable while the sash is out. It merely needs to be pulled! The bolt type is usually used in pairs, and to lift the sash you pull on both simultaneously and lift at the same time. If the bolts are not in good order, or if the wood is damp and swollen, they will stick, and you will need a third hand to cope with the situation. If this becomes too aggravating, the bolts can be replaced by a more modern arrangement. This consists of a pair of coil springs in a metal case, together with metal straps that are fastened to the sash. The springs are inserted in slots in the upper part of the jambs, and they work just like sash cords and weights. On the other hand they are almost invisible, and no one is likely to notice them.

If you wish to make the top sash so that it can be raised or lowered, all you need to do is to cut the step on the jamb strip a little lower and drill a couple of holes in the jambs for the catches. It is not advisable to have the top sash opening the full depth. It is too easy to accidentally drop it level with the lower sash, where the spring catches cannot be reached, and have it stuck there. A foot of opening at the top is ample for most purposes.

Since the sashes and frames are almost always painted, you do not need to make repairs and replacements out of old wood. But nowhere is it more essential to use well-seasoned stuff that will not warp, shrink, or swell. This type of window is very difficult to make airtight, and well-fitting storm windows are essential for winter use in cold climates. If an old window is eliminated for any reason, be sure to save both the wood and the glass for possible repairs and replacements.

In painting the windows it is always best to remove the sashes and paint them separately. All the edges should be given one good, smooth coat, and the insides of the jambs also. The sash should not be replaced until there is no danger of sticking.

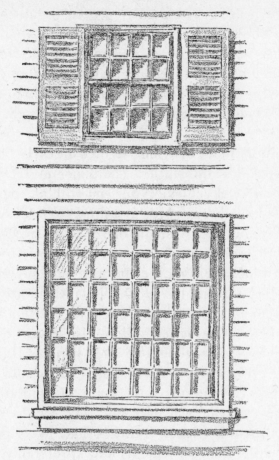

Large windows can sometimes be used effectively if the balance is preserved.

### Adding New Windows

In any house that has not been brought up to date you will probably need to let in more air and light by adding windows or by increasing the size of those that already exist.

New windows should be added with extreme care so as not to spoil the outside appearance of the house. If possible they should be of the same general style and proportions as the original ones, particularly as regards pane size. This does not mean that all new windows should be exactly the same size as the old ones, or even at the same height from the floors. We know of several old houses whose window sills are at varying heights, but the difference is unnoticeable from the outside. Under some circumstances such variations would appear quaint rather than objectionable, but it is best not to call attention to them by boldly outlining the windows in color or adding blinds that, being closer together, would emphasize the difference.

With the simple types of windows used in early houses there are rarely any mechanical difficulties. The major problems lie in determining the best way of achieving this end without spoiling the house inside or out. Generally one of the first things to be decided is whether to add a new window close to an old one or to replace the old one with something much larger.

If the principles governing the structure of a braced-frame house are understood, you should have little difficulty in determining where a window can go and where it can not. The question is then largely one of appearances. Internal conditions also govern the placing and size of the windows. Sometimes one large window is better than two smaller ones because of the way the wall space would be broken up. In other instances the reverse would apply. If ventilation is not to be considered, a second window would probably serve better than a large single one. On the other hand, a tiny or narrow room can be made to seem much larger if a very wide window, preferably recessed, occupies a large part of one of the side walls.

All of these things and other specific circumstances have to be taken account of, and the alternatives weighed, and no one can decide but yourself. Fortunately, in deciding, you have certain principles to guide you—repeated *ad nauseam* throughout these pages—in the matter of charm and atmosphere. Your pane size is set if there are other windows on the same floor and visible at the same time as the new one.

If there are no other windows on the same floor the panes may be made larger, because they will not seem out of place with smaller ones on the floor above or below. But the contrast must not be too great. Modern plate-glass windows are, of course, taboo. Nothing will spoil the architectural feeling of the house more surely, for reasons already explained. In this connection we have had cause to do considerable experimenting with large windows overlooking views. And we are quite satisfied that a view can be enjoyed as much through a set of small panes as through a large one, and without bringing the whole outdoors indoors, as picture-window proponents (abetted by the glass manufacturers) so passionately urge us to do.

With the small panes, indoors is kept indoors, and outdoors left where it should be, and the charm of the old-time room is not lost among the trees and grass. But in using any kind of large window we have to remember that it affects the scale of everything near it. A big window put close to a doorway will make the doorway look smaller. It may change the apparent proportions of the entire wall of the house. The scaling is therefore a matter for an architect who has enough tricks up his sleeve to disguise and disarm any untoward results.

Another point to be remembered is that two windows cannot be put very close together if they both have blinds. Sometimes this is achieved by having the adjacent blinds overlap. Properly done, this not offensive. But the windows cannot be put so close that the middle blinds must stick straight out from the wall, inviting a good strong wind to tear them off. Nor is it permissible to leave the blinds on one side of the window only, unless they are really large enough to cover it. The result is as "cute" as it is silly. Some get around this difficulty by hinging the shutter in the middle so that it folds upon itself.

Dormer windows present problems of their own, and a great deal of caution has to be exercised in adding them. The whole balance of the house can be ruined by dormers that are too little or too big, or badly proportioned, and by those that are improperly placed or the wrong style for the house. Usually it is best to play safe and put the new dormers on the back of the roof, and so preserve the original appearance of the front of the house—unless you have a definitely

Georgian house. The Georgian is the one style that usually needs dormers to give it that authentic Colonial appearance. But they must be of the proper kind, high and narrow and crowned with a simple pediment.

Before deciding on any dormer it is as well to do some measuring and see what actual benefits in the way of light, air, and space you are likely to achieve. Few dormers add anything to the usable space in an attic. The first thing to be determined, therefore, is just how much space you have to begin with. Under a sloping roof a great deal of the floor area is useless. A simple way of checking this is to attach a plumb bob to a line four feet six long and hold the end of the string against each rafter in turn so that the bob just touches the floor. This will indicate the points at which a wall four and a half feet high will strike the rafters and the floor. Chalk marks can be used to lay out the indicated floor space and the points at which the dormers will open out of it. The dormers give headroom and a small triangular space at ceiling height. But you have to be careful that the ridge of the dormer does not come too high on the roof. The floor space the dormers add is rarely usable except for a trunk or a small piece of furniture. In the larger ones you may be able to put a low dressing table or chest or even a comfortable chair close to the light.

In a gambrel roof there is usually enough headroom close to the rafters to permit the use of a very shallow dormer, with hardly any wall below it. On the other hand, in a roof that has a very low pitch the dormers need to be so deep and the floor space is so limited that very little air and practically no light gets in through them. The only satisfactory solution there is the continuous dormer which gives full headroom and adds that much more floor space. Unfortunately, unless it is very carefully designed, such a dormer will ruin the appearance of the roof and make the whole house look topheavy. If it is necessary to use such a dormer, it should be made as short as possible and hidden on the rear slope of the roof.

The set-in dormer, which is formed by extending the front wall of the house up through the roof, has the dubious advantage of raising the eaves line. For a squatty house this may be a help, but this type of dormer needs to be used with discretion because it breaks up the roof in a most untidy manner.

As explained earlier, there is a type of roof structure that interferes with the addition of dormers. Accordingly you should carefully examine the roof framing of your house before you plan any further. A heavy purlin beam used as an added support to a wide roof may be at such a height as to interfere with the dormer opening. This purlin should not be cut into without proper arrangements being made for its support at both sides of the break. This is a matter for an engineer or an architect to decide.

# CHAPTER XII

# Door and Shutter Hardware

## *Hinges*

TO MANY people the old-time door hardware is of even more interest than the doors themselves. This is not hard to understand, for in this handmade ironwork the eighteenth-century craftsman was at his best. Nowadays a hinge is a hinge like any other, but each old-time hinge was a creation in itself, with no two exactly alike. Today they are collectors' items, as many an empty old house with its doors lying on the floor after a visit from some ruthless connoisseur can testify.

People who know nothing about old houses will go into raptures over a pair of original butterfly hinges or an old HL. The so-called strap hinges are not quite so popular because only the student of such things can recognize their fine points and tell the old from the new. Nevertheless the strap-pintle hinges which were the commonest of all in 1700 for external doors—except the wooden or cowhide ones that you are not likely to run across in a month of Sundays—are often things of beauty, too.

At the pintle end of the hinge the metal is thicker and forms a loop by which it is hung on a vertical pin called a pintle or gudgeon. Even here there are differences. On some hinges the loop is narrower than the flat part of the hinge next to it. In some it is the same size, and on others it is wider.

The two principal means by which you can tell an antique strap hinge from a modern one are the way the eye is formed and the shape of the nail holes. In the very old hinges the eye into which the gud-

[ 158 ]

geon fits is curled around into a cylinder, and the metal tapers in thickness to the end. The thin end of this curl is not welded solid to the body of the strap. On modern hinges the eye is an almost perfect circle and is the same thickness throughout. Moreover it forms a perfect union with the strap, and no end of the curl can be detected.

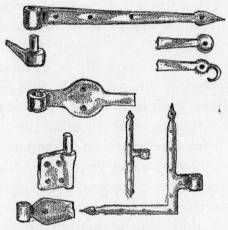

Some common types of pintle-
strap hinges.

The very old hinges were made to be fastened to the door with handmade nails. In some cases, especially on very heavy doors, the hole nearest the eye was made extra large to receive a large-headed spike or a rivet. The distinguishing features of the older hinges, however, are that the holes are unevenly spaced and irregularly shaped. They are smaller than those made for screws, but the most important point of all is that they were punched through the metal instead of being drilled. The difference is at once obvious in their shape and the distortion of the metal around them. They do not have the regular clean appearance of the drilled hole.

Most old-time strap-pintle hinges were cut out of sheet metal, and consequently they are thinner than modern ones, with square edges and flat ends. The very large old hinges were forged out of bar iron, but modern ones often are thicker and may have chamfered edges both on the strap and the end, especially if it is a point.

In the strap-pintle hinge the local blacksmith often gave full play to his fancy. Even when the hinge is unadorned by tricky ends the proportions may be so delicate and the workmanship so fine that it is a joy to the eye. Some of these hinges were not more than a foot long; others were two and a half feet or more, extending the full width of the door. And they were just as carefully made for the woodshed as for the front door of the house. In not one of them will you find a trace of a hammer mark.

Some of the hinges taper gracefully from the eye to the end. In others the blacksmith stole the architect's trick of making the edge look straight by giving it a little outward swell, or entasis. Some were boldly swelled, the taper increasing toward the end. But it was the end itself to which the blacksmiths gave the final distinctive touch. Here the hinge flattens out to receive the last nail hole in its center.

The three common types of ends were the spearhead, the rat-tail, and the thumb-end, though there were a great many fancy variations. And here again individual craftsmanship left its mark in the proportions and their relation to the rest of the hinge, and some are so distinctive that an expert can tell from which part of the country they come. The spearhead pointed straight like the hand of a clock. The rat-tail —not to be confused with the rat-tail cabinet hinge—was made in the same way, but the point was given a sweeping downward curve. In the thumb-end there is no point and no sweep. It is just squashed flat and spread in a rough oval, a broad side turned to the hinge.

The pintles were made in a variety of ways. One type was formed of a separate round pin clamped into the strip of iron bent around it to form the spike. The spike part in this type shows the joint between the two ends of the metal. In another type the whole pintle seems to have been forged out of one solid piece of metal. Still a third has a shoulder formed around the bottom of the pin to form a bearing surface for the hinge.

These pintles appear to be dated in the order in which we list them, the first-mentioned being the oldest. But this is not absolutely certain for all parts of the country. The pintle was driven into a hole drilled into the doorjamb, and the hinge fastened to the inside of the door. On all doors that open inward the hinges are on the *inner* side. Imitation hinge straps fastened to show on the outside of the door are therefore an absurdity.

On barns and woodshed the hinges are on the outside because the doors open outward. Small hinges of this type were often used on inside doors, though other and lighter types of hinges were favored before the advent of the butt hinge in 1783. In an attempt to provide

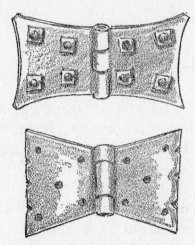

Dovetail or butterfly hinges.

a hinge that was more decorative than the strap-pintle hinge, some unknown genius introduced the snake hinge. This is merely a strap hinge with a double curve, but few smiths copied the idea. Much more popular in the early days were the strap-pintle hinges made in the form of an L or a T in order to hold the parts of the door together better and to prevent sagging. These are called angle-strap hinges.

A hinge known as the half-strap was used on house doors during the same period as the strap-pintle hinge. It was somewhat similar to the strap, but instead of a pintle it employs a flat strip on which a hinge pin is formed. This plate, shaped like a short section of the strap, was fastened to the doorjamb. Some authorities call this short member a braced pintle.

For interior doors and cupboards the decorative butterfly hinge was used as late as 1750. This hinge got its modern name from its shape. In the old days it was called a dovetail hinge. The two halves of the hinge are usually equal in size, though not always. They vary in shape, some having more irregular outlines than others, and many are decorated with notches along the edges of the wings. In the early part of the eighteenth century carpenters with an eye for color often slipped pieces of red leather under the nailheads. This enabled them to be driven tight without bending the thin metal or distorting it. It is to be feared that very few of these hinges will be found in houses today for reasons recounted earlier.

A modified form of the butterfly hinge was known as the tomahawk or hatchet hinge. This was practically the same as an H hinge except that the upper part of each leaf was shaped like a butterfly wing. Each leaf therefore looked in outline something like a miniature tomahawk. This type of hinge is even more rare than the butterfly.

Much more commonly used on houses after 1750 were the famous H and HL hinges, a vast number of which have been salvaged to date, though you may have difficulty in finding them. These, like the others mentioned above, were made of wrought iron and were very flat and thin. Though they were obviously handmade they showed no hammer marks. And they did not, as the modern commercial imitations do, look as though they had been stamped out of sheet metal. In the earliest ones the holes were punched for nails, but during the last quarter of the eighteenth century the holes were often made larger for flat-ended screws and some attempt made to countersink them. After 1800 they were all made that way, even though cut nails were sometimes used to hold them.

Some of the H and HL hinges were made more decorative by having the ends of the metal serrated and the body scored across with two or three lines. Those that had three lobes formed on their ends are called the clover design. A great many of these hinges were made in this country, but for a long time they were imported in large quantities. For room doors the hinges are usually a little over seven inches high and made from metal strips one inch wide. Much smaller ones are used on cupboards and inside shutters.

The HL hinges were specially valuable for use with framed doors, the L portion helping to keep the frame from sagging and the joint from coming apart. The H hinges, on the other hand, could very well be used on solid doors, where the L type would be of no special advantage, and support the center of a door which had an HL top and bottom. In view of the prevalent vulgar custom of painting these

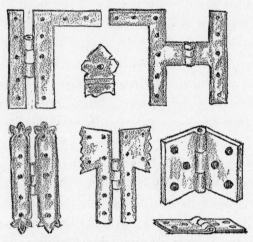

H, HL, hatchet, and butt hinges.

hinges black, and thus turning an artistic feature into an eyesore by exaggerating it, it seems necessary to call attention to authentic usage.

Before the days of interior paint, which varies in different parts of the country, from 1740 to 1770, interior woodwork was left unfinished. Naturally the ironwork, too, was left as it came from the smithy. It was not jet black, but a much softer tone containing a tinge of red that did not clash with the wood. When it became common practice to paint doors and woodwork, the hinges, likewise, were painted over with the same color. They were still visible but not obtrusive. Since the H and HL hinges only date from the 1750s, they will generally be painted over, and so should they be today. Nothing is so disturbing to the eye as to enter a room painted white, with every closet, cabinet, cupboard, and room door dotted with these odd-shaped splashes of black. Good taste demands that they be toned down.

The next popular type of hinge to be introduced was the butt hinge, which was, and still is, used on both the interior and exterior doors. Technically the butt hinge is any hinge which is intended to be applied to the edge (or butt) of a door instead of the face. When the door is closed the leaves of the hinge fold back upon one another and only the back edge is visible from the back of the door.

This type of hinge is much more easily illustrated than described. The earliest of these hinges, which began to be used on house doors about 1740, were made of wrought iron, with all the characteristics as regards holes and finish of the other earlier types of hinge. They were a development of the square cabinet type of hinge, which was applied to the face of doors just as the still earlier butterfly hinges were.

These cabinet hinges, much used on drop-leaf tables, were made of very thin pieces of iron folded double around the hinge pin. The edges of the two layers were then welded together. Such flat hinges were used on furniture as early as 1725, and it is possible that the first butt hinges were made in a similar manner. They are, however, very rare.

After 1783 the butt hinges began to be made of cast iron. Square and ugly, they were an uninteresting forerunner of the coming industrial age.

## Latches and Catches

The one item of door hardware that really gave the old-time smith an opportunity to express himself was the house-door latch. There is little doubt that the earliest designs of thumb latches were copies or adaptations of those used in England, just as the knocker latches were of Dutch origin. Nevertheless, in both cases, the American craftsman soon left the imprint of his genius upon them. The variety of designs seems only to have been limited by the imagination of their creators.

Some of the most popular designs of thumb latches used in the New England colonies in 1700, and after, were designed long before that time. And many a latch hammered out on an early-eighteenth-century anvil is still giving good service today. The wrought iron of those

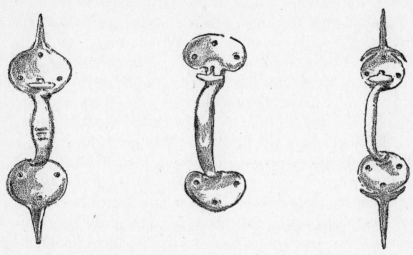

Suffolk latches of the ball-and-spear, bean, and swordfish designs.

days was remarkably pure and did not easily rust. Instead, by continuous use it acquired a glaze or patina that is both beautiful and one of its most easily recognized characteristics.

The typical early latch consisted of five parts—a looped handle called a grasp or pull; a broad thumbpiece with a flat extension that passes through the door, called the lift; the bar, which is a flat strip of iron several inches long, with a hole in one end by which it is hinged to the door; the staple, which straddles the bar and keeps it from moving too far in any direction; and the catch, or strike, that forms a notch in which the bar rests when the door is closed. The strike, of course, is fastened to the doorframe. The most decorative feature of the latch is almost always the flattened portion at one end or both ends of the handle, by which the grasp is nailed or screwed to the door. These parts are called the cusps, and the earliest designs are by no means the simplest.

Practically all the door latches used on small houses of 1700 to 1826 were of wrought iron, and very few indeed were of brass. During this period a large quantity of English hardware was imported; nevertheless a great deal of it was produced by local blacksmiths,

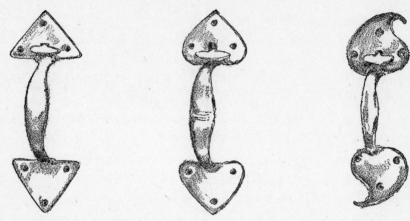

More Suffolk latches of the arrowhead, heart, and tulip designs.

especially in the inland towns and settlements. This is often evident from the characteristic designs which are peculiar to certain localities, as in the case of hinges. In restoring old houses these differences have to be kept in mind, and the type and design of latch used that is common in that area. To use a latch of definitely Pennsylvania design on a house in Maine, for example, would be an obvious error, though it must be admitted that there are precedents for such a course. Early settlers moving from one part of the country to another did on occasion either take their hardware with them or made it according to designs used in the part they came from. Such "foreign" types of latch, however, are not likely to look as though they belonged on houses typical of another region.

The two types of old latches most frequently seen on the early Colonials are the Suffolk and the Norfolk. The Suffolk appears to be the common type, the other being little used before 1800. The immediate noticeable difference between the two types is that the Suffolk latch has a separate cusp at each end of the grasp, while in the Norfolk latch the handle is fastened to one long back plate or escutcheon.

From the seventeenth century on, the Suffolk latch was used all over New England, in New York, Pennsylvania, and Virginia. In the westward migrations many of these latches were taken along, their characteristics betraying their origin. The cusps, naturally, display the greatest variety, but there are several other important differences in the constuction of the individual latches, some of which are useful in dating them.

In the earliest type of Suffolk latch, the bar lift passes through a slot in the upper cusp, where it is held in position by a tongue formed on the underside of the lift. This is called the cusp-lift type. In later examples the tongue is replaced by a shoulder or slot formed in the lift, but the tongue type was used also till the end of the eighteenth century. Long after the introduction of the cusp-lift type of latch came the swivel lift. This has a thick vertical extension between the cusp and the handle, through which the lift passes. The lift is held in place by a pin which passes through it and the sides of the slot.

There is also a great deal of difference in the design of the lift and the thumb press. In the oldest latches the thumb press is thin, flat, and either round or oval in shape. The next development was the hollowing or dishing of the press to fit the shape of the thumb. A highly controversial feature is the shape of the lift, which appears in many forms from the earliest times. A great many of them were curved, some slightly and others in almost half a circle. Conversely there were many others that were straight and projected an inch or less beyond the bar. It has not yet been determined which came first, and why. One theory has it that the long lifts were unpopular because they caught and tore people's clothes. But in some areas, notably in Pennsylvania, short lifts are found on most of the older houses. Whatever the truth of this, the fact remains that the short lift was soon found useless for opening a tight door and some other means of pulling on the door had to be provided. This occasionally took the form of an extension on the end of the bar, perhaps in the shape of a loop or a right-angle bend. In other examples a small knob is welded on.

There are many other variations in the design of the bar, chiefly in the matter of decoration. The pivot end, for instance, may be made to match the ends of the door hinges, but in the small, unimportant houses the straight, tapered bar is almost universal.

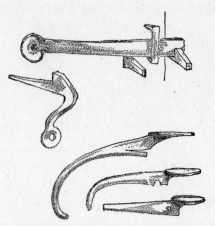

Details of Suffolk latch—lifts, bar, staple, and catch.

Except in the matter of size, nearly all staples are simply a piece of flat metal, with pointed ends that are bent over so that they can be driven into the wood. But now and again one turns up that is mounted on a plate which is held to the door by nails. Another rare type that is held by two nails has no back plate. The catches occur in a variety of shapes. Mostly they consist of a lipped spike that is driven into the wood. But many are stiffened by a brace extending downward from the head. This brace end is flattened and nailed to the jamb. Extra decoration may have been secured by twisting the brace. Very late ones may be mounted on an escutcheon plate.

In spite of all these variations in detail, it is the cusps that hold the greatest interest and tell the most. Because there are some hundreds of designs in existence, it is quite impossible to catalog the features which tie them to any particular locality. The best we can do here is to illustrate a few of the representative types. The better-known designs of cusps are the bean, the tulip, heart, arrowhead, the swordfish, and ball-and-spear. Besides the individual designs of cusps, some of the Suffolk latches have a cusp only at the upper end. The lower end of the grasp then is drawn to a point, driven through the door and clinched. Most of this type seem to have originated in Pennsylvania. Other latches have large cusps at the top and small ones at the bottom,

A Norfolk latch, and a Blake's patent cast-iron latch.

and, finally, some have no cusps at all—just short, flat extensions of the handle pierced for nails!

The Norfolk latch is, on the whole, much less interesting than the Suffolk type, but there are more of them on doors today. The commonest design, which almost everyone must have seen, consists of a long, rectangular plate, with semicircular pieces cut out of the corners; often with a cast-iron handle, and the lift pivoted between flanges that stick out from the back. Those made in the early 1700s were considerably more decorative, though they look stodgy beside the Suffolks. The more attractive ones cut down the width of the escutcheon and make the top and bottom parts look like cusps.

The earliest Norfolk latches were apparently all handmade and had handles of wrought iron. In the latter part of the eighteenth century, however, they were imported on a large scale, and these are obviously factory-made. One difference was that the early types had straight lifts and flat, round thumb presses. After 1800 most of them have curved lift ends and dished presses, and those of 1825 or later always have escutcheon plates on the bar pivot, the staple, and the catch. The bar also may have a knob riveted or welded on. Between

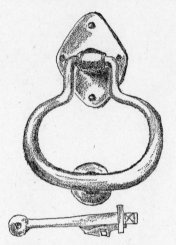

A Dutch type of knocker latch.

1800 and 1840 the Norfolk latch gradually superseded all types. But in 1840 it, in turn, was swept off the country's doors by Blake's patent cast-iron latch.

### Knocker Latches

Wherever the Dutch went they seem to have taken with them the Dutch door and the knocker latch that goes with it. These latches go back into antiquity and were used all over Europe in the sixteenth century. Those brought to the embryo America were of two types, one peculiar to the Dutch settlements, which lifts the bar by a cam, and the simpler type, found all over New England, in which the handle turns the bar directly. By reason of its construction the Dutch

[ 170 ]

type is much easier to operate and will open weather-stuck doors that the other kind will not.

Both types employ a round or stirrup-shaped handle passing through the eye of a pin which connects it to the operating mechanism. The bottom part of the handle usually is thickened to concentrate the weight where it will do the most good when used as a knocker. With some of them, a striking button, like an oversized

Four types of Colonial knockers.

nailhead, was driven into the door, in others a heavy protective plate was nailed on, if it did not form part of a large escutcheon. The illustration of a common design of the Dutch types will convey far more than any amount of description

## Knockers

Knockers were never so universally used in this country as they were elsewhere, and most of the surviving ones are found on town houses. The earlier ones were of wrought iron and were similar in appearance to the ring or stirrup latch handles. Others consisted of a single or Y-shaped bar pivoted to a plate. But the knocker did not really come into its own insofar as decorative value is concerned until late in the eighteenth century, when brass ones became popular. Some cast-iron knockers of classical design were used on later Georgian and Greek Revival houses.

## Locks

As early as 1730 latchmakers began experimenting with locks. The first steps in this direction were the use of a large metal plate to which

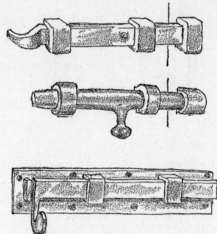

Three early Colonial door bolts.

the latch bar and staple were anchored, and the use of a spring to snap the bar down. By 1825 latch locks were common, and both the earlier drop handles and brass knobs were used to operate them. Somewhere in between these dates the sliding lock bolt was combined with the latch, the bolt being operated by a key. Locks, of course, are very old, and rare examples of wood-cased ones have been unearthed in America dating back to the seventeenth century. With these old locks go very interesting and often ornate escutcheons that may very well be used to decorate the keyholes of old houses today.

## Bolts and Bars

Sliding iron bolts were used to fasten doors throughout the eighteenth century, but many householders preferred to reinforce them with a stout wooden bar. The bar was generally a stiff piece of oak or ash, around two by four inches in size, held in a large iron staple at one end and in a similar hook at the other end. In places where iron was scarce the early doors had wooden bolts that worked in a hole drilled or gouged in the doorframe. You are not likely to run across many of these, but the wooden bars are still used in many houses built before 1750. By that time iron bolts were the accepted means of securing outside doors.

The simple bolt used on small houses during the eighteenth century was often no more than a piece of flat iron held by two staples and sliding into a third staple on the doorjamb. Sometimes a small peg or knob served as a handle. At other times the end of the bolt was turned up to form a grasp. Some very old bolts consisted of a thin iron rod, with a knob welded in the middle. The slenderness of these safety devices is amazing, considering the weight of the doors they were intended to hold. The better-made bolts were mounted on iron plates attached to the doors by nails. Apparently this type also was employed throughout the 1700–1850 period.

### Shutter Fasteners

The remaining pieces of house hardware which should be mentioned are the shutter hinges and fasteners. The hinges range from the strap-type, used mostly on solid shutters, to the lighter angle and offset types for louvered blinds. Most of the latter types are cut out of sheet metal and are flat and thin. The pintles usually were of the spike type and driven into the wood, but many of the later ones were mounted on plates and held by nails or screws. After 1800 a screw type of pintle was introduced.

The fasteners were made in an enormous variety of designs, to hold either the bottom or the side of the shutter. The majority of them were pivoted so that they hung vertically, those holding the side of the blind being made in an L or T shape. Any straight piece of iron would have served the purpose in most cases, but here was an opportunity for decorative work that the craftsman could not miss. The pivoted fasteners were made in all shapes and sizes, from flat straps with curled ends to S-shaped creations of twisted square iron. In some instances plain hooks were used as fasteners, and elsewhere ingenious contrivances enabled the blinds to be regulated from inside the house. These fanciful contraptions, however, should be of little interest to the small-house owner, who will, most likely, have to be content with the simpler and quite effective balanced shutter fastener, if he uses that type at all.

Wrought-iron shutter fasteners.

In the nineteenth century a great many of the shutter fasteners of the type described above were replaced by spring-type hooks screwed into the border of the blind. These were used almost exclusively on houses and wooden wall coverings, and snapped into a screw eye attached to the wall.

In the restoration of old doors and shutters by the addition of metalwork contemporary with them, the first rule is to make sure the design is authentic for the period. This you can do by reference to any of the standard works on the subject listed in our bibliography, or by a visit to a museum of American antiquities. The second point is to confirm the fact that the design is indigenous. And both of these will leave you plenty of latitude for the satisfaction of your aesthetic taste. But steer clear of the run-of-mill commercial imitations of old-time hardware. The good ones need no paint to give them a mellow look, or carefully applied hammer marks to show that they have been faithfully copied by hand from an old original. Labored imitation is worse than frank and honest indifference to authenticity.

# CHAPTER XIII

# Hearths and Chimneys

NO MORE sturdy a piece of construction was ever attempted by our forefathers than the chimneys they put in the Early American house. The southern-style gable chimneys were substantial enough in all conscience, but the central chimney's foundations were monumental. Assuredly those early masons must have been kin to the builders of the pyramids. The smallest foundation of this type that we have examined was six feet square, the largest twelve feet, and even larger ones have been known to exist. Eight feet, however, seems a good average size for the small house.

Invariably the chimney bases are built of stone—either field stone or ledge rock, but rarely, so far as we have been able to observe, is quarried or dressed stone used in these houses of modest size. In the earlier houses the stonework may be carried up as far as the attic and the chimney top finished off in brick. Those that are of stone to the very top may logically be suspected of being older than those with brick tops. This, however, is not always the case, especially when the top stones are dressed. In later times, when bricks were more plentiful, the brickwork was carried farther down. In two houses that we examined, one built circa 1765 and the other in 1775, bricks were used from the ground floor up, with stone filling behind them to the top of the kitchen fireplace. From there on up, brick was used exclusively.

In the earlier eighteenth-century house the foundations of these chimney stacks are usually of stone laid in lime mortar and filled with rubble. In order to bond the masonry together it was customary to lay

an occasional wooden beam in the wall. If you examine these beams
you will often find that they are mortised, or show other signs of having been used for something else before they were built into the chimney. They may, as a matter of fact, have been part of a house built long
before yours, or even of a house that stood on the same foundations.

Later chimneys may have an opening near the base through which
you can see the interior. This quite often consists of a circular brick
lining which goes up as far as the first floor and is covered with a huge
slab of stone. No one seems to have discovered the purpose of this

The massive base of a central chimney with
fireplace cradles.

construction. In those days wood ashes were valuable for the making
of soap, lye, and potash, and it is possible that it was intended for an
ash pit, connected by an opening with the hearth above. But in those
we have examined no such opening was visible. In some cellars there
may be a fireplace, particularly if one side of the cellar is at ground
level. In such cases there will probably be evidence of a room having
surrounded the fireplace at some time. Such cellar fireplaces are rare
in houses built before 1750.

Just below the cellar-ceiling level there are usually two heavy
wooden beams set in the chimney masonry, extending along two sides
of the chimney base, their ends projecting so as to form supports for
the main-floor beams. On two, or sometimes three, sides of the base
there will also be cradles to support the hearths of fireplaces above.

[ 177 ]

Occasionally one of them will serve as a foundation for a brick oven. Each cradle is usually formed of a pair of heavy timbers, their bottom ends set low in the chimney base and their top ends framed into a sturdy beam at the first-floor level. Thick boards are laid on these outward-sloping timbers and rubble piled on top of them. Above the rubble lies the hearthstone of the fireplace above. The hearthstone may be anywhere from three to nine feet long and two to seven inches thick. In many parts of New England these hearthstones are of marble, though in one recorded instance an old tombstone was used, lettered side up!

As many as seven separate flues have been found in a central chimney stack. But it was a far more common practice to connect all fireplaces into one large flue, especially in the early days. Sometimes these fireplace outlets were carried up a considerable distance before joining the main flue. In others they were connected well below ceiling level. Some chimneys that we have examined are divided in two by a brick partition, forming separate flues for the upstairs and downstairs fireplaces.

Where the great stack breaks through the roof it may be four feet square or more. Early ones were likely to be oblong, with the long side parallel to the ridge and probably behind it—but this is not conclusive evidence of antiquity. Where rooms and fireplaces were added after the original structure was in place, there may be an extra flue bonded into the stack above roof level. Two or three of these would convert the original stack into a pilastered chimney of considerable decorative value, but this rarely happened after the seventeenth century.

In the 1840s, when airtight stoves were all the rage, a conspiracy was set afoot to destroy these monuments to New England colonial domesticity. Builders and insurance men combined with stove manufacturers to abolish the huge chimney and replace it with a piddling, spindly brickwork stump that ruined the architectural unity of the house and made it look ridiculous. Too often they succeeded in this nefarious design, and today many a long and skimpy Victorian chim-

ney springs from a noble stack lopped off at first-floor height. This is
a remnant worth looking for in a house that has a suspiciously insignificant chimney topping its broad roof.

In the southern colonies the masons were no less keen to have their
works survive for posterity. Each end chimney of the small houses
served fewer fireplaces than did the central stack, and it was accordingly less massive. On the other hand, the foundation and lower part,
whether of brick or the rarer stone, were sturdy enough to withstand
loads far greater than any the tall stack would be likely to impose
upon them, even in a hurricane.

Most of the early chimneys were of brick throughout, while later
ones used stone for the foundation. Whether the house was of brick or
wood, the chimneys were built outside the gable walls. From their
broad bases they were narrowed down, as they climbed toward the
roof, by successive sloped weatherings and offsets. These changes in
dimensions took place in both width and thickness, in contrast to the
New England outside chimneys, which were usually the same thickness throughout and reduced only at the sides.

In one or two of the Southern Colonial houses still standing—one
being in North Carolina—the chimneys are kept flat at the back by
spacing the upper part away from the house wall. From the second-
floor ceiling level on up, such a chimney stands free. More often than
not, the early southern chimneys have a separate flue for each floor.
Occasionally two fireplaces on the second floor might share a flue, as
when they are set back to back, diagonally across the corners of adjoining rooms. Where there are separate fireplaces in front and back
rooms, the custom was to build separate chimneys, even in the smaller
houses. Apart from these idiosyncrasies, the chimney structures were
similar to those of the North.

Some of the northern end chimneys were built inside the house
structure, often forming part of the gable walls. If the entire gable
was not of the same material—brick, or more commonly stone—the
masonry would be confined to the chimney and back wall of the fireplace.

The tops of chimneys form an interesting subject of study in themselves. In the warmer climates, where there are no cold winds to whistle down the chimneys, the stacks are finished off with one or more courses of bricks corbeled out as decoration. In the colder parts, which include a large section of Pennsylvania, the chimney tops are

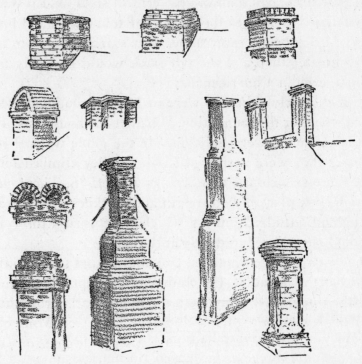

Common designs of chimneys from the North and the South.

often covered. This covering may range from a simple, flat flagstone, supported on three thicknesses of brick, to an arched brick hood. Large chimneys may even have a double hood, and we have seen the same thing in both Maine and South Carolina, which is one exception that proves the rule. In northern Ohio we made note of a big hood, semicircular in shape and made, apparently, of tin! If the proportions of a plain chimney will stand one, a hood is a good thing to have. But, if possible, you should follow local custom in the type you adopt.

They are a help in windy country, especially if the flue is big and the hearth is wide.

Another custom prevalent in the South, and which seems to have persisted for a very long time, is that of painting the chimneys white. Occasional examples of this are seen today on old houses in the North. Legend has it that when the American Tory sympathizers wanted to advertise their loyalty to the Crown, they painted their chimneys

A late-eighteenth-century kitchen fireplace with bake oven
and wooden mantel.

white with a band of black around the top. Whether accentuating the chimney in this manner helps the house architecturally or not depends upon individual circumstances. But there is authority for doing it, if you wish to do so, and no one will accuse you in these times of disloyalty to the Republic. On the other hand, it is a rather dressy finish for a modest house.

## The Fireplace

The early fireplaces were built of roughly dressed stone, but later it became the custom to face them with brick. As the century progressed, the kitchen fireplaces were made smaller and more compact. In houses already standing, the cavernous openings were sometimes reduced in size by being partly bricked up. This often occurred when the kitchen was moved to a lean-to and a new fireplace for cooking was added there. The fireplaces in the other rooms were comparatively small, and even these were sometimes reduced in size in later years. Shortly after the Revolution, when the famous Count Rumford published his theories on fireplace construction, many fireplaces were given sloping backs and sides made shallower and provided with a smoke chamber and shelf in the flue.

Upstairs fireplaces were usually supported on timbers built into the chimney stack or on floor beams bridged across to carry the hearth. The smaller fireplaces were very often formed of stone slabs, especially at the sides. The side slabs usually were dressed smooth on one end to form the face of the fireplace. While both heavy wood lintels and huge stone ones were used in the large fireplaces, stone lintels were commoner in the small ones. When bricks were used for the sides of the fireplace they sometimes had wood blocks set in them, and the lintel may have consisted of a wood beam faced with a slab of stone. These things require careful checking on account of the fire hazard.

The fireplace openings were decorated in a variety of ways. Some of them were faced with soapstone or marble, or even with Dutch tiles. Delft tiles were used as early as 1725, and later, copies of Dutch tiles decorated with local scenes were produced in some sections. As far afield as the Midwest decorative iron plates have been substituted for tiles.

Another decorative adjunct to the fireplaces, large and small, was the cast-iron fireback. This was a large iron plate bearing some fanciful design and often the name of the maker and foundry. It was placed against the back wall of the fireplace, or even set into it, to protect the brick or stones from direct contact with the flames. It was also believed that it was effective as a radiator of heat.

Probably the best-known of these firebacks are those made by the famed "Baron" Stiegel at his foundry near Lancaster, Pennsylvania, in the middle of the eighteenth century. Other firebacks, however, were made even earlier in Saugus, Massachusetts. These plates can be used to advantage in almost any fireplace. The difficulty is to find one outside a museum!

Much more frequently found in these old houses is a fireplace mantel. The mantel is the wooden frame that surrounds the fireplace opening. The early large fireplaces had no mantel at all. After 1700, however, wood paneling on the fireplace wall was common, and a thick, heavy molding, called a bolection molding, framed the opening. Above it there was often one large panel, flanked by smaller ones. In later houses a shelf was perched on top of the molding, forming a mantelpiece or mantel shelf. The shelf should not be confused with the overmantel, which was a narrow strip located much higher than the usual mantelpiece.

Most mantelpieces first blossomed out on chimney breasts between 1725 and 1750, when plaster took the place of paneling on the other walls of the room. It was during this period that the fireplaces of Georgian houses were made smaller. From then on, up to Revolutionary days, mantels became more ornate and elaborate, especially in the best room of the house. The year 1725 also witnessed the flowering of the custom of building cupboards in every possible nook around the fireplace. In some houses these were merely open shelves, but most house owners seem to have preferred that they be fitted with doors—particularly the "parson's" cupboard which held the toddy bottle!

Occasionally one of these cupboards would have another cupboard behind it, concealed by a movable panel. Other hiding places for valuables were located behind the mantel paneling, or in a nook over the chimney back which could be reached by raising a tread of the stairs. Some nervous householders even went so far as to hide their jewels in lead boxes underneath the hearthstones. Those chimneys in which the flues were joined by brick arches, too, afforded space for cupboards hidden or otherwise.

Smoke chambers or smoke ovens also were compartments recessed into the chimney, but these served a more prosaic purpose. Hams and bacon could be hung there for curing. Such accommodations have been found beside the chimney in the kitchen, on the stair landing, and in the attic. Not all of them got their smoke from the kitchen fire. In some instances the attic smoke chamber was built on later, at a point where the chimney was corbeled back to a smaller size before reaching the roof. These had floors of wood or tin and held receptacles in which smoke-producing wood could be made to smolder. This

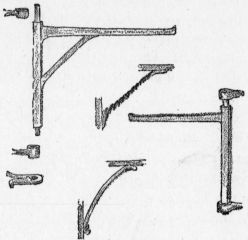

Authentic styles of fireplace cranes and sockets.

arrangement was popular for a very long time in country districts. One such was added in 1873 to a house we know of that was built in 1749!

No old-time fireplace was complete without something to hang the cooking pots from over the open fire. By 1700 the crane was well established in this capacity and continued to serve many a family till well into the nineteenth century. The typical crane consists of an inverted, L-shaped wrought-iron bar, usually with a brace across the angle. The vertical part of the crane has rounded ends which fit into a pair of iron sockets or eyes projecting from the masonry in one side of the fireplace. The crane, hinged in this manner, is able to swing out into the room, if necessary, or to be swung back over the fire.

# Hearths and Chimneys

The point to be noted, if you need to install one of these cranes in place of one that has been removed, is that the crane is detachable from its moorings. A friend who tore out one of the anchors to install his crane was much embarrassed when he was shown how simple it all was. For others who have not already discovered the trick, we may explain that the upper rounded end of the crane is much longer than the lower one, and the eyes are very little closer than the total length of this upright bar. To install the crane, you insert the upper end into its eye first and lift it as far as it will go. Then you drop the lower end in its socket. It's as simple as that! An assortment of iron pothooks hung on the crane, or, perhaps, an adjustable trammel completed the ensemble!

In a very old house you may find a strong iron hook driven into a ceiling beam over the center of the fireplace. This was to support a hempen string from which meat was hung for roasting. The string would twist back and forth, occasionally helped by the cook's fingers. A set of two or four similar hooks, set a little farther back from the fire, were probably intended to support a bar from which the wash was hung to dry on rainy days. These are atmospheric touches it is best not to disturb.

## The Oven

A description of the old-time fireplace would not be complete without reference to the bake oven. The first bake ovens were built into the back of the fireplace, and not until 1775 or thereabouts did they begin to appear at the side of it. As a rule they were then provided with a short flue connected to that of the main fireplace. In many instances the oven was added long after the fireplace was originally built.

To many of us the bake ovens are one of the most interesting and sometimes puzzling features of any old-time kitchen fireplace. Some confusion undoubtedly arises from the common practice of calling the brick oven a Dutch oven, there being two other baking devices which have a much better claim to that name. The point is clarified more fully in the Glossary, but this brief note will explain why we adhere to the term "brick oven" or "baking oven" in this connection.

The bake oven, then, is always built of brick, though rubble may be used to fill the odd spaces behind and around it. The usual type of oven had a floor of brick and only rarely of stone. The roof was arched in front, and the much wider circular back end was domed. It is said that this dome was constructed of rectangular bricks by first filling the bottom of the oven with wet sand and molding it to shape. Bricks, well mortared, were laid over the sand and left to set. Then the sand was taken out. The oven was closed by a square of tin that fitted into the opening where it was held by a flange in the brickwork.

The method of using the oven was to light a fire of small wood inside it. When the bricks were hot, the ashes were swept out and the food was put in. At first only the oven appeared at the side of the fireplace, but a little later a second opening was put in below it. This was a handy place to store the hot wood ashes while baking. At other times the space formed a useful receptacle for the special wood used in the oven, and perhaps a cooking utensil or two.

The baking ovens were usually three feet from the floor and about eighteen inches across the opening. The interiors vary in size, some of them being large enough to bake two dozen loaves of bread at once! The shape of the oven changed as the fireplaces grew smaller. Instead of being round they became oblong in shape, with an arched or barrel-vaulted top instead of a dome.

In later years a plain batten door covered both the oven and the storage pit below, but after 1800 some houses had a heavy cast-iron door over the oven and left the other opening uncovered. Occasionally the inner door of tin continued to be used in conjunction with the iron door. Quite frequently we have come across batten doors that have been used on ovens that had no tin cover. As a result the doors are badly charred. Some of them were charred at the bottom also, indicating that the used ashes had still been hot when the door was closed. It hardly seems likely that such a door would actually catch fire, but there is a great deal of evidence that defective bake-oven flues were one of the prime causes of the old houses burning down.

In houses with end chimneys the bake ovens were often so long that they extended out beyond the wall, projecting either into a lean-to or shed or into the open air. Some of them were corbeled out, top and bottom, while others rested on a brick foundation, the brick tops

In end-chimney houses, bake ovens sometimes projected beyond the outside wall.

being domed so that the whole thing looked like an old-fashioned beehive. Such a top was very often stuccoed over to protect it from the weather. In Pennylvania we have seen them with roofs built over them.

Soon after the beginning of the nineteenth century stoves began to take the place of open fires in many sections of the country. As a result houses built from 1816 on frequently made no provision for fireplaces, except in the kitchens. The stoves needed nothing more than a simple flue, and in many houses that was all that they got. The chimneys were built, inside the house or out, no more than six-teen inches square, just large enough to take a four- or five-inch stove-pipe!

This was the era in which the small Greek Revival houses blossomed forth with a pair of spindly chimneys, and perhaps a third one at the back to serve the kitchen. The same sad fate befell many an Early American-type house also, and today these houses lose much of their attractiveness for the house hunter because they have no fireplace. What is worse, in many instances, the chimneys were placed between windows or in other locations where it is quite impossible to substitute a fireplace for lack of room. The only thing that can be done under these circumstances is to start anew and put a fireplace where none was before. Since a chimney will be needed for the furnace, it may be possible to use that built for the kitchen.

Before taking such a drastic step as building new fireplaces, however, the possibilities of a Franklin stove should be considered. The wood-burning stove is not only attractive in appearance but leaves the fire exposed to view. In fact it has many of the advantages of the fireplace, plus better and more economical heating capacity from the fact that it brings the fire out into the room.

Sometimes the stoves are used as fire frames and built into brickwork. But they do not even have to be located against a chimney unless a yard or so of stovepipe is objectionable to the eye!

### Chimney Restoration

An old chimney is one thing that *must* be restored and made safe regardless of any other considerations. More fine old houses have been burned to the ground through neglect of this precaution than from any other cause. Practically every old chimney leaks. You have only to go up into an ancient attic and look at the chimney stack to see how bad this defect can be. If green wood has been burned, as it so often is, the outside of the chimney will be streaked with resin that has condensed in the flue and leaked through cracks in the bricks and holes in the mortar and run down the outside. Such chimneys may be caked with resin and the holes full of it. And when an extra-hot fire is started in a fireplace the resin begins to burn. The whole chimney takes fire, and the burning resin and hot gases leak through to the woodwork and floor and roof, and soon there is nothing left worth salvaging.

Even without the resin there is plenty of dust, and natural tinder baked over the years that can smolder unseen till it gets the air it needs and suddenly everything is ablaze! Fortunately for the wise householder such chimneys can be made perfectly safe. A thorough inspection of the chimney, therefore, is the first thing that should be attended to, preferably before the house is occupied.

In addition to the defects due to decay of the mortar from weathering and neglect, and cracks developed through the settling of the house, there may be even more serious ones caused by accident or carelessness. For example, if a chimney catches fire the first impulse of the householder is to dump a bucket of water down it or squirt water from a hose or extinguisher up it. Any liquid poured into the chimney while it is hot will inevitably crack the brick or stonework. It may even split the upper part of the chimney in two. And this may have been done before the house came into your possession!

Such damage, therefore, is the first thing to look for. If the chimney is large, the mason will be able to get down it. But first of all it should be decided whether or not that part of the chimney above the roof is in good enough condition to remain undisturbed. This can be examined, both inside and out, and the condition of the brick or stone and mortar checked. At the same time the dimensions of the flue should be measured, for the only way to make it absolutely fireproof is to line it with tile or concrete or enameled steel. If the upper part is defective it should be rebuilt. Taking it down for this purpose will save a lot of trouble in inspecting the rest of the flues.

Usually the top is taken down to the level of the attic floor and sometimes still further. This enables it to be rebuilt an inch or two larger in both directions to accommodate a lining tile. But before even an inch is added to the girth of a chimney it is as well to see where the inch will go. We vividly recall the predicament of a friend who rebuilt her chimney top, only to find that it made her already very narrow stair landing an inch and a half narrower. She thought nothing of this till she came to sell the house and found that several of her prized pieces of furniture could not be got down the stairs! Luckily she was able to sell them to the new owner of the house.

Even if the chimney seems to be in perfect condition it is always best to play safe and line it throughout. The usual method is to start from the lower end and apply a good coat of plaster made of lime, sand, and a bit of cement to the chimney throat and smoke chamber. This is generally simple to do if there is no fireplace damper in the way.

The next step is to install angle irons across the flue, by bedding them in the masonry. These serve as a foundation for the lining. The new lining will probably be quite a bit smaller than the flue, and the space between them will have to be filled in with concrete made of broken brick, lime, and sand. If round tile can be procured, so much the better. A round flue is more efficient than a square one because of the whirling of the smoke as it ascends. In a square flue the corners check this whirling action and interfere with the free flow of the smoke and hot gases. For this reason a round flue works just as well as a square one of the same dimensions.

A simple method of installing a lining, which may be used without disturbing the brickwork, is to lower a round metal pipe into it. These pipes are coated with a refractory material, unaffected by heat. The space around the pipe is plugged with concrete as in the case of the round-tile flue lining.

In estimating the relining possibilities it is necessary to determine how many flues the chimney will be called upon to accommodate. All flues should be lined, and they will draw better if they are carried up independently to the top of the chimney. If there is a brick partition in the chimney, this can very easily be removed to make room for the regrouping of the flues. If certain fireplaces are not likely to be used, or only used infrequently, they may share a flue with another fireplace, provided the unused ones are equipped with dampers to shut off the air. The area of a flue, incidentally, should generally be no less than a tenth of the area of the fireplace opening.

# Hearths and Chimneys

One of the first problems you will have to face in allocating the flues will be what to do for the furnace. The local mason's solution is usually to punch a hole through the bottom of one of the ground-floor fireplaces for the furnace pipe and stop up the fireplace. A much better plan, very often, especially if you object to losing the fireplace, is to put up a new chimney on the rear side of the house exclusively for the furnace. This permits the insertion of an ashpit at the base of the chimney, and the whole system can be kept perfectly clean and dust-free.

If the old, deep fireplaces are in their original condition, they will probably need to be made shallower and have new facings applied to the cheeks. At the same time it is well to examine the brickwork around the opening. Either the bricks or the mortar may be crumbling from the combined effects of heat and age, and there may be a hidden wood lintel that needs replacing. Note should be made also of other wood inserts in the brickwork, and the chimney throat measured for a damper. Since it is the proportions of the fireplace that determine whether or not it throws out the heat but not the smoke, it is best to leave this reconstruction to an expert, merely supervising the work to see that nothing is done to spoil the old-time atmosphere of the fireplace.

Very often it is possible to buy old brick for the new fireplace lining, failing which, good common brick will do, particularly for the sides. For the lower part of the back, firebrick or tiles are often used in the facing, but these are rather out of keeping with a Colonial fireplace. Instead you can use oven-burned brick which will be dark and show signs of glazing. This lining should be only one brick thick (four inches), so that it can be renewed at any time without disturbing the rest of the fireback. The original bonding of the bricks should, of course, be copied. One important point is to bring the sloping sides (the cheeks) forward to within four inches of the face of the fireplace. This means that the facing bricks cannot be laid as headers down the sides.

One other thing about the fireplaces that may need attention is the hearthstone. If it is tilted so that part is above the floor level or part below it, the remedy is usually simple. Since in ground-floor fireplaces the stone rests on a bed of rubble, all that is needed is to raise the stone and regulate the height of the rubble or the sand that is probably laid over it. If the stone is very large and cracked, it can be relaid to close the crack and leveled so that it is not unduly notice-able. Such a crack is most often caused by spilling cold water on the hot stone. But sometimes, in the course of years, vibration causes the sand, and even small rubble, to trickle out through the cradle boards and leave a hollow space beneath the stone. Then all that is needed to produce a crack is to bump a heavy piece of furniture on it. In resetting a stone, therefore, it is a good idea to check the entire bed and see that the stone is supported throughout its length.

Upstairs hearthstones are much smaller and much less likely to be abused. Also they will probably be bedded down more solidly, since there is so little space between the boards that support them and their undersides. Adjusting or relaying them, consequently, is a rare neces-sity and a simple matter at worst.

# CHAPTER XIV

# Steps Up and Steps Down

FEW features of an old house are so directly concerned with comfort and convenience as the stairway. And still fewer present such variety in their construction, location, and decorative value. Old-time stairs of the small house vary all the way from a narrow, steep, enclosed straight run to a leisurely, open, and winding staircase with ornamental balusters and decorated stringers. And the stairs are important because they not only provide access from one floor to another, but frequently determine the efficiency of the heating system. Very often they also decide whether or not that chaise longue, or the massive chest that was grandmother's, goes on the second floor or the first. More than one family has had to have its principal bedroom on the ground floor because the furniture simply would not go up the stairs!

All of these things have to be taken into consideration before deciding what, if anything, is to be done with the stairs. In the central-chimney style of house the stairs are almost always located in the front porch or entry. Sometimes they climb straight up behind the kitchen flue and over the parlor fireplace. In this position they are usually, in their original condition, boxed in between the parlor wall and the chimney. A door at the bottom of the stairs, and sometimes one at the top as well, would take care of any drafts.

Another popular arrangement was to run the stairs up alongside the chimney, with a right-angle turn at top and bottom. This stair might be open or closed, but the majority of those that we have seen have had balusters instead of paneled sides. Getting anything up or down an enclosed stair of any type is a practical impossibility, and ingenious methods were sometimes used to overcome that handicap. The most interesting arrangement that we have encountered was a trap door in the old kitchen ceiling (now a living room). That, of course, would be possible only with an unplastered ceiling. Other schemes included hinged or removable panels on the staircase and a collapsible rail at the top of a stairway. In one instance the secret was not discovered until we had removed several layers of paint and paper from a stair partition. This revealed the fact that the boards had at one time been sawn through, in step fashion, for a distance of several feet. Still another stair had two removable steps to provide the necessary headroom.

The modern idea, of course, is to take out an upstairs window to get furniture in. This works well unless the windows are all too small. In one instance we found that a new window had been installed next to the old one, leaving what was practically a broad mullion between them. This mullion had been made removable, and when the windows were taken out there was a space almost five feet wide.

The straight stairs usually are too steep for comfort, their angle being limited by the room doors at the foot and head and the chimney or bake-oven brickwork underneath. On the other hand it often happens that a few extra inches can be stolen by bringing the foot of the stairs farther forward and moving the top step farther back. This may be sufficient to reduce the height of the risers half an inch or so and increase the tread correspondingly. And even half an inch makes a big difference to the navigation problem on such a stair.

One reason for the bottom step having been pushed back may have been the need for clearing the front door. In such case extra space can be contrived by replacing the single front door with a double (two-leaved) one.

Far more hazardous, as a rule, than the steep straight stair is the winding stair that has "winders" instead of platforms at the turns. The winders, or triangular steps, are so narrow at the inside of the turn that the only safe place to step on them is close to the wall. And that side rarely has a handrail!

So many of these old stairs have beautiful moldings and panels and wonderful worn steps and handrails that it seems almost criminal to disturb them. But sentimental considerations can hardly be allowed to outweigh the risks to life and limb in a badly designed staircase, and occasionally we have no alternative but to rebuild them.

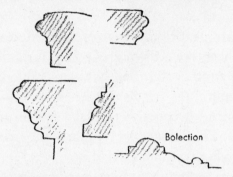

Early-eighteenth-century staircase moldings.

In the winding stairs the problem is to replace the winders with platforms. This means an extra step, or even two or three. If the extra steps can be worked in at the top or bottom, the middle part of the stairs, between the upper and lower winders, may possibly be left undisturbed. In any case the first thing to check is the top and bottom steps, which quite often have lower risers than the rest. Beyond this the problem is similar to that of the straight-run stair.

Some stairs end in the old kitchen, perhaps with a door over the bottom step or just in front of it. This offers a possibility of securing extra stair length by bringing the bottom step right into the room. It may enable you to substitute a platform for winders. The only possible drawback is that the platform may have to be on a level with the top winder, and this very often reduces the head clearance below the permissible minimum. Apart from this, some staircases are built that way and lend a note of interest and novelty to the room.

The most interesting stairs, without doubt, are the open ones which are common to all styles of house. The very early ones had what was known as a boxed string, the outer ends of the steps being covered by a wide molding. The side of the stair below the string was boarded or paneled in. The first stairs of this type had no balusters, but they did have a handrail supported by square newel posts. Soon after 1700

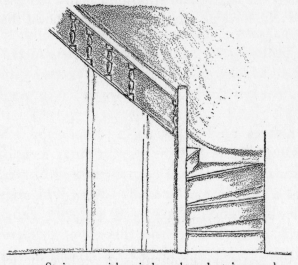

Staircase with winders, boxed string, and
short balusters.

the carpenters began putting turned, short balusters between the rail and the string. The number of these balusters was a matter of choice that had nothing to do with the number of steps. Both square and turned newel posts were used. The next development was to take away the high boxing and expose the ends of the steps. Longer balusters were necessary, and these were let into the treads of the stair. In the smaller houses there were usually two balusters to a tread, and only occasionally were there three. And although square balusters were sometimes met with, the turned variety was more generally used in the East. But in Ohio and points west the square type of baluster predominated.

Though stairs in the front entry were a feature of most central-chimney houses, there are some in which the stairs are found in the rear or lean-to portion of the house. In this position they may not be so crowded and therefore be not so steep. Usually they come down against an end wall of the house and turn at right angles at the bottom with a platform instead of winders.

With houses that have an extension built on, there is often another staircase leading up from this part to the room or attic above it. There may then be a doorway through the dividing wall giving access to the original part of the house. Such a stair will invariably be a secondary one, probably steep and enclosed. Where such a stair exists it is preferable to adapt it to the ingress and egress of furniture and leave the principal stair in its original condition, provided it is not dangerous.

In central-chimney houses that are a century and a half old or more it is highly probable that the stairs already have been altered from their original design. In many cases they will have been taken out entirely and a new form of stair substituted. For example, many of the old entries had a straight stair, with a closet occupying the rest of the little porch, and a door on either side giving access to the rooms. It seems to have been quite common practice to tear out the closet and remove the door to one of the rooms. Then by changing the straight stair to one with a turn at the bottom it makes an imposing inside hall open to the one room. Unfortunately this not only spoils the character of the room but brings the front door into it and plays hob with the heating.

The best thing to do in such a case is to restore the original arrangement. If this involves adding two doors to the room—one to the entry and one to the closet—the change may not be altogether for the better from the standpoint of appearance and usable wall space. In such a case you could very well compromise by putting the closet door in the entry. This will present you with the happy alternatives of replacing it with either paneling or bookshelves. Book space is usually the better choice because the touch of color that books give is always helpful in a room that has a great deal of woodwork. But be sure to use old wood for the bookcase. Even if the rest of the woodwork is painted, old pine makes a fine setting for the books and will not look out of place.

In the central-hall type of house the stairs are, almost without exception, located in the hall. And in practically every instance they are of the open-string type, often consisting of a simple, straight run. And since they have ample room to stretch themselves, they are invariably less steep than those of a central-chimney house. In some of the southern style of Early American houses there was a transverse hall which necessitated the use of stairs with two right-angle turns similar to those of the central-chimney house. As a rule, however, these halls were wider, and the stair could be made without winders.

In the first of the small Early American houses the only entrance to the cellar was outside. Later, as cellars were made larger, the space under the stairs was utilized for steps down to the cellar. When secondary stairs were installed in the kitchen of central-chimney houses, the cellar steps were very often moved to that location. When this has been done, you will have much greater latitude in remodeling the main staircase. And, of course, if it has not been done, you can probably do it yourself.

Cellar stairs, because they cannot be seen from the living quarters, and being little used in comparison with the main stairs, are often crudely constructed, steep, and rickety. Generally they consist of no more than rough boards laid on a pair of carriers. This would be quite satisfactory if the boards were firmly attached and the carriers braced at the sides, preferably against a wall, so that they could not sway. Risers are not necessary, but they do add stiffness and solidity. And if there is a problem of cold air sweeping up from the cellar, both risers and enclosed sides, together with a door at the bottom, are a tremendous help. In any case, adequate lighting of these steps is of first importance.

The stairs up to the attic are also of the simplest type and generally closed. In the lean-to house they may go up from one of the rear rooms, but in the central-hall type they are usually placed over the main stairs. Ordinarily they will require little or no attention, unless they are in bad condition or the paneling is so thin that they require insulating. Insulating these stairs is usually a very good idea anyway. Occasionally you will find a closet built under them that limits the headroom of the stair below. This headroom should not be less than seven feet six inches; if it is, the remedy is obvious.

The height of the step risers in cellar and attic stairs matters little, within limits, but it is of first importance in a main staircase. A steep stair is fatiguing for anyone, and for elderly people and children it is dangerous. The maximum height of any step should not exceed eight and a half inches, and the nearer it approaches seven inches the better. So long as the over-all height of the stairs remains the same, and the over-all length (the "run of the stairs") is unaltered, the rise and the tread will govern one another. If the rise is low, there will be more risers and therefore more and narrower treads.

A really comfortable stair has risers of seven to seven and a half inches and treads of ten inches, but in these old houses this is rarely accomplished. The Georgian and other hall-type houses offer the best opportunities for an easy stair, but usually there is some limiting factor to be considered. The formula that the modern carpenters follow is to make the two dimensions, rise and tread, total between seventeen and eighteen. Thus, if the riser is eight inches, the tread will be nine or ten inches. But formulas are of little use in making easy stairs fit restricted spaces, and the points discussed so far may indicate the possible solutions.

The stair steps in the small houses were often of very simple construction. The edge of the tread and the riser finished off flush where they met. In other instances, the tread projected slightly over the riser. In order to take the fullest advantage of the width of the tread, the front edges were not rounded off to form a nose as they usually are today. This blunt nose gives the steps an old-time appearance which should be preserved. In order to get a wider tread, the nose was made longer so that it extended beyond the riser, perhaps as much as an inch and a half. This was about the safe maximum, because any more overhang than that would be likely to catch the toe of a person ascending the stairs and trip him.

Some carpenters left the joint between the tread nose and the riser plain. But others stiffened it, and at the same time added a decorative touch, by putting a cove molding under the overhanging tread.

In actual construction stairs varied a great deal. The simplest stair consisted of a pair of carriers on which the treads and risers were laid without any side pieces or stringers at all. Such stairs were used between partitions and usually only for secondary or attic stairs. If the stairs were wide, say three feet or over, the carriers would probably be set in six inches or more from the ends to give firmer support to the middle of the treads. Such stairs often had carriers no more than an inch thick, the width depending on the depth to which the steps were cut into it.

Another early form of stair had carriers composed of heavy beams, say six by four. These were not cut at all, and only the back ends of the treads rested upon them. The risers stood on the treads, and horizontal support for the treads was provided by diagonal pieces, about two by one and a half inches, pegged to the beams and set into the tops of the risers. There are a number of variations of this system, but they are rare, and the type of stair you are most likely to find in your house will have both carriers and stringers.

In the normal stair of this kind, the stringers are flat boards about one by twelve. A pair of carriers, cut out of two-by-ten planks, are nailed to the inside faces of the stringers. These carriers are notched to support both the treads and risers. Various kinds of woods are used for the steps, the most usual being either oak or pine. Sometimes the treads will be of oak and the risers of pine. These may be three quarters to one inch thick, the riser often being of slightly thinner wood than the tread.

It was customary with this type of step to lay the riser first, so that the back edge of the tread butted against it. The riser was then nailed to the tread from the back to give it extra support.

Common defects of the old stairs are looseness of the boards and squeaky treads. Both of these may arise from the springing of nails due to flexing of treads from heavy traffic. Carrying heavy furniture up and down stairs, for example, may well bend the treads in the middle. This lifts the ends and loosens the nails. Renailing will help in all cases where the nails are put in from the top. If the risers are nailed into the treads the backs of the treads or bottom edges of the risers may

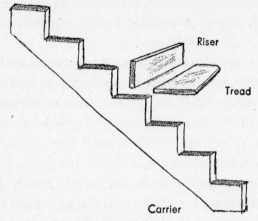

Riser

Tread

Carrier

Principal stair units.

have split. Renailing will not help here, but wooden blocks fastened to the carriers will make a better and more permanent job. These blocks may even be used to hold wide oak strips under the backs of the treads where they meet the risers. This will help even if the riser is above the tread, and in either case long screws through the strip into the riser are advisable.

The causes of looseness and squeaking are usually the same, and curing one will eliminate the other. For desperate cases corner blocks may be nailed and glued inside the angles between the tops of the risers and the treads that rest on them. Warped or flexible stringers may also give rise to these symptoms, and this is best handled by fastening two-by-fours to them below the steps if there is room. Sometimes the only real solution is to make another carrier, at least two inches thick, and install it under the center of the treads.

Usually there is nothing that can be done about the width of the stairs. Theorists tell us that a stair on which two people can pass needs to be at least three feet wide, and preferably three feet six inches. But such stairs are rare in old houses, and even if they were not there seems little need in such short flights for the impatience which passing on stairs suggests. Getting bulky objects up and down is, of course, another matter. But it is astonishing how big a piece of furniture can be got up a stair two feet nine inches wide. We have, more than once, insinuated a large easy chair up a stair that was only twenty-six and a half inches from wall to wall!

The finish to be given to stairs is not altogether a matter of personal taste. In some small houses built around 1700 to 1725 the wood was often left raw. Sometimes it was given a coat of homemade paint. In open stairs where the risers are immediately obvious both bare wood and light-colored paints are objectionable. The reason for this is that unless the steps are covered with a runner they will soon be streaked with blacking from people's shoes. On narrow treads, particularly, it is hard to avoid marking the risers, and the only palliative is to make the riser dark to begin with. In the late eighteenth century most of these stairs were painted white, except for a panel of dark paint down the center. The white paint is helpful on enclosed stairways where the lighting is poor. On the open-type stair it became the fashion in some areas, around 1800, to paint or stencil floral designs on the risers. The background was usually a neutral tone such as medium gray. The effect was delightful, and people were more likely to step carefully so as not to spoil the decoration.

# CHAPTER XV

# Paints, Plasters, and Old Nails

PAINT made with milk or strong beer, and plaster laden with cow hair are two old-time materials that we can very well do without in this day and age. But in restoring our old Colonials we do need to adhere to the authentic colors and wall textures, or at least be able to match them. Likewise, in applying our hardware and nailing down our floors we can with advantage, decoratively speaking, use the handmade nails and screws, or reasonably accurate facsimiles thereof. Furthermore it will be a distinct advantage in helping us to visualize and understand the qualities and colors of the early paints and plasters if we know how and of what materials they were made, just as a brief glance at nail and screw making will show us the reason for their peculiarities.

Not much painting of houses was done before 1725, either inside or out, and any paint that was used was homemade. Long after that time there were still house owners who did not hold with newfangled notions and refused to hide their weathered pine sidings under a coating of glue and chalk. Their faith in the weather-resistant qualities of the wood evidently was justified, judging by the number of old unpainted houses that have survived to this day. On the other hand, the majority of citizens liked a little color in their lives and while they were painting their barns mixed enough to do the house over as well!

The earliest paints were water colors, often made with skim milk, which need not surprise us in these days of casein paints. Marion Nicholl Rawson gives one interesting paint receipt that is characteristic of those pioneering times. This called for a pound of potatoes, skinned and baked, then mashed in a third of a gallon of boiling water. This soupy mixture was strained, and two pounds of powdered chalk and half a gallon of water added. "This mixture," the receipt states, "will form a glue to which any coloring matter may be added— even charcoal, brickdust, or soot. It is cheap and durable for barns and fences."

In the very early days the choice of coloring matter was limited and depended a great deal on the locality. In many places there were natural deposits of minerals, such as iron ocher, suitable for making paint, but elsewhere people had to rely on vegetable products and their own ingenuity. One of the earliest wall coatings of which there is any record was whitewash, and it was used as a "preservative against dampness and moss." This early calcimine was burned and powdered limestone "slacked" in water.

The most popular color of house paint, for a long time, was Venetian red. This was made by burning yellow ocher (limonite), then grinding the red clinker into powder and mixing with skim milk. The yellow ocher was used for a similar paint called pumpkin yellow, which was slightly higher in the social scale than the red, doubtless because the latter was largely used for barns. At any rate, by 1750, when white lead began to be available for making an oil paint, people were painting their houses white. Those who could not afford to do the whole house painted the front white and left the sides and back either yellow or red. But as late as 1757 others preferred to make their own white paint—especially in the country districts—with ground "water-lime," though they usually made a concession to progress by adding a little linseed oil.

When, in the middle of the eighteenth century, painting became the thing, many who were in a position to do so grew their own flax so that they could extract the linseed oil from its seeds. Thus in time oil took the place of skim milk, water, and the "strong beer" that was sometimes prescribed. Fish oil, too, became available in many places, and apparently worked just as well as linseed oil. At the same time other minerals were gradually being added to the list of coloring materials, eliminating the need for putting nails into the dye pot to get a rust color or using beet juice for the red.

By 1745 a great many colors were available, such as grays, greens, Spanish brown, yellow, and combinations that make gray-green, blue-gray, etc. The greens used for shutters and blinds were made at first from verdigris (copper acetate) and verditer (copper carbonate). By 1800 many painters obtained a variety of greens by mixing gamboge (which some called gumbugiam), with varying proportions of indigo, or verditer, or by combining yellow ocher with indigo. A rather incomplete list of such materials available at that time would include: verdigris, yellow ocher, Venetian red, white lead (mostly imported from England), gamboge, verditer, red lead, vermillion, dragon's blood (a dark red tree resin), umber, and Prussian blue.

The white lead, however, was the most important ingredient, and this did not become generally available till after the Revolution. At that same time colors in powder form were produced in quantity, together with zinc oxides (which make a whiter but not so durable a white paint as white lead does), raw linseed oil, and turpentine.

The use of white paint for the outsides of wooden houses and the wood trim of stone and brick ones became universal. This was the so-called Colonial white, but some few still preferred grays or yellows for the body color. Green was the favorite for shutters, as it has been ever since. But the first white-lead works in America was not established till 1809, when Samuel Weatherill erected one in Philadelphia. He produced white lead in paste form, and users made up their own paints by adding powdered color, linseed oil, and turpentine.

Paint was used for the interiors of small houses almost from the beginning of the eighteenth century. Housewives apparently found it difficult to keep their baseboards and wainscoting clean and were reduced to protecting the woodwork near the floor with a coat of color. Black or dark red paint was applied in a broad band the width of a baseboard. This band of paint was usually carried entirely around the room and even applied to the bottoms of the doors. The black was made with lampblack or soot, and the red was generally a mixture of one of these with Venetian red. This dark, rich red became quite popular as time went on, and in some parts acquired the name of Indian red. It was used on peg boards and other places where a decorative touch was needed. Another early attempt at decoration was to whiten the ceiling between the beams and daub or dot this over with black. In some instances this combination was reversed and the white laid over the black.

The earliest method of treating wood surfaces was to rub them with raw linseed oil and sometimes wax them afterwards. But, as oil paints became practical for even the small houses, the custom of painting both panels and floors rapidly spread. Many an early kitchen floor was brightened with a coat of yellow ocher, but the favorite wall color was the blue-gray of which we find so many examples today. If you have occasion to take down an old painted board to the bare wood, you will often find that the first coat of paint is a blue-gray and almost as hard as iron.

Not till 1745 or so did the use of other colors for interior walls become at all popular. In this period the paneling of Georgian houses, always more pretentious than the Early Americans, was likely to be painted in any one of a variety of colors—blue, green, yellow, gray, or red. In the Southern Colonials it soon became stylish to use two tones in the same room, and often the molding and panels were finished in contrasting colors.

In the majority of small houses throughout the country the use of paneling diminished rapidly throughout the eighteenth century, its last refuge being over the fireplaces. Even there panels gave way to plain boards, and boards sometimes also formed a dado around the kitchen or common room. The increasing areas of plaster were a great temptation to traveling artists and decorators, and in the late 1700s stenciled walls spread a like rash over New England, upper New York, and as far west as Ohio. Wallpapers had been introduced into the homes of the wealthy in 1735, but they were imported from England and France for many years after that and remained expensive. Consequently few small-house owners could afford this stylish and decorative protection against dampness.

In later years quite a few citizens plastered newspapers on their walls, and some of them even went to the trouble and expense of covering the newsprint with hand-blocked designs and coloring them. Until 1790 the wallpaper was made in small pieces—18 × 15 inches, 18 × 18, or 20 × 28—all of it printed by hand from blocks. By 1800 a small amount of wallpaper was manufactured in this country, but most of it was still being imported. The first wallpapers were so thick and tough that they could repeatedly be taken off one wall and used on another. That is why we have been able to salvage so many examples of this early work.

Hand blocking did not die out till 1840, when wallpaper-printing presses were built, though the machinery was not perfected till 1867.

Many of the early papers were printed in subdued colors, principally browns, grays, and greens. But it was not long before someone came along with the more spectacular and less desirable (from our viewpoint) flock papers. These were made by printing the design in boiled linseed oil. While the oil was still "tacky" a fine woolen dust called "flock" was blown across it. This made the design figures look as though they were made of felt. As if this were not bad enough, feathers, silk, and fur also were used as a substitute for the flock!

In the early days the papers were attached to the walls with a paste made of rye flour and sugar. But this was too dark and heavy, and in later times wheat paste came to be used instead.

Today there are a great many reproductions of the old wallpapers available. But none, we hope, of the flock type! In selecting these papers for use in old houses it is as well to get designs that are of the proper period. For example, there is one particularly delightful pattern in brown and green which incorporates a male figure attired in pantaloons and conical hat. These were fashions of 1815 or thereabouts and would not be wholly suitable for an eighteenth-century house. Another paper best avoided in small Colonials is the typical French paper of the Colonial period, such as the fleur-de-lis design, or, indeed, any highly formal paper. Likewise modern, whimsical patterns should be avoided even for the kitchen. Paper, as a matter of fact, is best reserved for the bedrooms and parlor. Whitewash still has a great deal to recommend it as a foil for old wood and even for framed pictures.

## Plasterwork

In looking over old houses that have been restored we are frequently discouraged to find that the plasterwork is a horrid sand color. And, in all probability, it will be finished very roughly, with trowel marks so exaggerated as to be obviously deliberate. A plasterer of any period would have to try hard to turn out work so crude. Much of the responsibilty for this lack of authentic treatment of the plaster seems to lie with the plasterers themselves. But they can hardly be held to blame when all the instruction they get is to plaster "in the old-fashioned style." The result is something we, at any rate, have never yet encountered in examining the plaster of old houses, even as far back as 1683.

As early as the seventeenth century plaster was made from lime, and lime was made from shells, and later from limestone. And in all cases it was white. Before 1700, and especially in country areas, plaster was sometimes made of gray clay mixed with cattle hair and formed into a paste with water. This undoubtedly gave the walls a dirty-gray tinge, but there were few householders who were satisfied with that kind of plaster in its raw state. Whenever they were able to do so they covered it over with whitewash. In any case, by 1700 lime plaster was pretty generally available, plastered walls were common, and plaster was beginning to take the place of panels over fireplaces, though that did not become general till a century later.

The early plaster was a mixture of lime and sand, to which cattle hair was added as a binder. This kind of plaster was used in many places right up to the twentieth century. In the western states plastered walls were usual from the earliest times, because wainscoting had practically disappeared in the East by the time those frontiers were settled.

After 1800 another kind of plaster was sometimes used, principally in farmhouses. This was called pulp plaster and, as its name suggests, was made from tree pulp mixed with sand and water. However, you are not likely to encounter much of this.

Coincidental with the use of plaster came the employment of wood lathing to hang it on. This we discussed in detail earlier in connection with partitions. The point that concerns us here, however, is what to do in case replastering or patching is necessary. Naturally it is desirable to preserve as much of the old plasterwork as possible, even if it is to be covered with paper. But unless the plaster is firmly attached to its laths it might just as well be replaced first as last. The way to test for this is to tap the plaster with something solid. A hollow sound, indicating a gap between plaster and backing, is easily identified. Pressing the plaster with the fingers also may disclose a space by the movement of the plaster. The remedy here is to cut out the loose material and replaster. This chopping out of the loose plaster needs doing carefully, preferably with a sharp tool. Knocking it out with a hammer will probably cause further damage, yet that is what the average plasterer will do if left to his own devices.

If there are a good many loose spots, and the whole wall is in poor condition, it is best to strip it down. But it is rarely necessary to relath. It would, of course, be much simpler to do away with the old lathing and replace it with metal lath. And that is probably what the plasterer will suggest. Cleaning out the old plaster clinches from the laths is a tiresome job. There are, however, two objections to this course. One is that with modern lathing you will get a perfectly flat surface which will look like a new job for a very long time. The other is that removing the old construction is one more step toward eliminating everything that makes the house interesting in the first place. There is, actually, a vast difference between plastering done over old hand-split wooden lathing and that on metal lathing, or even sawn lath. This

# Old American Houses

shows up particularly on whitened walls where the reflection value is so much higher than that of paper.

In modern plastering there is no need to use hair. The lime comes in the form of lime putty, which is merely calcined lime that has been slaked with water. This is mixed with sand and water to the required consistency and is tenacious enough to stand by itself. Plasterers today usually apply the plaster in two coats—a ground coat and a finishing coat. The undercoat may be the lime-and-sand mixture or some standard preparation sold ready-mixed. The second coat may be a finish mixture such as lime putty and plaster of Paris (calcined gypsum). But it should not be as smooth and hard as modern walls. The required effect is easy to get, but it is not a simple matter to make it so that it will last. This calls for the services of an expert plasterer who will match the appearance of the existing finish.

Outside plastering, which we call stucco, was at one time quite common on brick and stone houses. Interesting effects were sometimes secured by grooving the stucco to represent blocks of dressed stone. If your house has an old covering of this kind it is best to preserve it, not only to maintain the character of the building but to secure the added protection and insulation it affords.

The original stucco was made of lime with a great deal of sand, but, strangely enough, the sand did not noticeably affect the color of the finished stucco. One result, therefore, of using the lime was a dead-white surface. On the Pennsylvania houses the surface coat of the stucco was applied by spattering with a broom. In New Jersey the popular taste ran to smooth walls, and the stucco was finished with a trowel.

This early type of stucco is supposed not to have been lasting, and this is given as an excuse for not duplicating the work today. But to our minds any wall covering that lasts fifty years, let alone a hundred and fifty, is long-lived and worth saving. The cements, which nowadays are substituted for plaster in stucco, do not have the desirable whiteness, and probably the best that can be done is to mix a little yellow ocher with the white cement. This will give an ivory tone to the stucco, which appeals to some and not to others.

# Paints, Plasters, and Old Nails

Using an ordinary cement, with a dash of ocher, produces the buff color that is seen on so many Victorian houses, and which is hardly to be admired. The alternative, of course, is to use plain cement stucco and paint it over afterwards. But a special paint is made for the purpose and should be used. It will probably require a new coat every

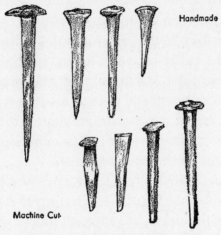

Handmade

Machine Cut

Comparison of handmade and "cold" nails.

year or so. Nevertheless, with all the new types of paints that are now being developed and introduced, it would be unwise to suggest that even these drawbacks will not soon be overcome.

## Nails and Screws

Handmade iron nails were used in house building throughout the eighteenth century. The first hand-wrought nails were imported before 1700, and later long strips of iron for making nails—called nail-rods—were made in England from fine Russian and Swedish iron and brought to the colonies in that form. Soon, however, rolling and slitting mills were established here which turned out nailrods in various weights both from imported iron and the bog iron found in many parts of the country from Maine to Virginia. So heavy did the demand for American nailrods become that the British Government found it necessary, in 1759, to order the slitting mills closed down. After the Revolution, of course, they became more active than ever.

The nailrods were cut and forged by hand into nails of the required size. The nail maker—who may either have been a professional or merely a farmer who needed a few spikes—heated the end of the rod, which was usually a quarter of an inch thick, and hammered it to the thickness and taper required. He then partly cut through the rod, inserted the end in a hole of the proper size in a swage block, and broke it off. The swage block was a heavy iron block with holes through it of various sizes, and it held the nail while the head was hammered into

This shows how nails were clinched.

shape. You may find nails that were made two hundred years ago still in good condition. The reason for their long life is that the purity of the iron and the density of texture, produced by hand forging, made the nails extremely resistant to rust and dampness.

The nails were made in a wide variety of shapes and sizes, from very large shipbuilding spikes to tiny brads used in furniture. Several different kinds of heads were used in house construction, and some of the nails had sharp points, some flattened ones, and others had square ends that punched out the wood instead of splitting it. Most of the nails were made very long so that they could be clinched over on the backs of boards.

The first patent for a nail-cutting machine was made to Ezekiel Reed of Bridgewater, Massachusetts, in 1786, but no machine-made nails were produced in quantity before 1795, these being troublous times. The machine-cut nails, sometimes called cold nails, were made of the same quality of iron as the handmade ones. They were strong and durable, but they lacked the toughness of the hot-forged ones and sold at one third the price of the handmade nails. Cut-iron nails were made in many varieties, both large and small, but most of them had square points, and to avoid splitting the wood they were driven in with their broad sides parallel with the grain of the wood.

In making over an old house a great many of the handmade nails can be salvaged, even if a half inch or so is lost in unclinching them. Old-house salvage organizations sometimes collect them, and we know of one man in that business who has several barrelfuls of these old-timers that look as though they might have been made yesterday. It is, of course, possible to get a local blacksmith to make the nails, but they are likely to be expensive. On the other hand, it is generally better to use modern nails than to adopt the modern machine-made imitation of the hand-cut ones which are no imitations at all.

Wood screws were made soon after 1700, but they were mostly used on furniture. Being handmade, without the benefit of steel dies, the cutting of the thread demanded both time and patience and no little skill. Consequently they could not be turned out in large numbers as nails were. The early screws were made from round iron and were not tapered. Their ends were cut off square, and the slots in their heads were rarely exactly in the middle. The threads, too, were uneven and rounded instead of sharp.

When once you have seen and examined one of these screws you will have no difficulty in telling the difference between them and modern machine-made ones. Since they had no points it was necessary to first drill a hole to put the screws in. If the hole is of the correct size, the screw will hold even better than a pointed one which spreads the fibers of the wood. That is why, even today, careful workmen will always take off the sharp point of a screw and insert it in a drilled hole. If new screws have to be used in restoration work, the shiny heads can be dimmed by the application of a little japan lacquer.

# CHAPTER XVI

# Removers and Refinishers

PAINTING a wood surface is usually a much simpler and more enjoyable process than removing the paint that someone else has applied. Particularly is this so in dealing with the very old paints, some of which seem to possess many of the characteristics of armor plate. In stripping down old wood we have often got as far as the first original coat which it was difficult to believe was paint at all. It not only looked like slate but felt like it, and ordinary paint solvents seemed to have no effect on it at all. Most old woods, on the other hand, are well worth cleaning off, especially if the first coat was an oil paint. The wood will, surprisingly enough, have a patina equal to that of an unpainted old wood surface. In fact one of the loveliest finishes we have ever seen on old pine was that given by a 150-year-old coat of Indian red, rubbed so thin that the grain showed clearly through it.

The logical way to arrive at a decision on whether or not to take a room down to the wood is to find out what the custom was in the days when the house was built. This, unfortunately, is very difficult to do because there never was any definite end or beginning to customs of this sort, especially after 1700. As a rule, however, it may be concluded that up to 1725 the chances are that the room woodwork was naked and unadorned. From 1725 to 1745 it would be doubtful, but after 1750 paint was most likely used. If you decide to remove all the paint, it might be as well to clean off a small test area first and see what kind of wood surface you have underneath. Sometimes, in these small houses, the wood was not particularly handsome and would not repay the time and effort involved.

# Removers and Refinishers

The principal reason for removing paint from old wood is to expose the original surface. If the wood is to be painted again, taking off all the old paint is generally a waste of time and effort, unless the whole surface has deteriorated in some way. Such a thing could happen by blistering, through being too close to a stove or fireplace. Normally, however, only the top coat or two need be removed, and very often nothing more than a gentle sanding is required. In every case the thing to guard against is the cutting of the wood surface either by scraping or sanding, and the burning of it by chemicals or heat. These things often happen when old-fashioned methods of paint removal are used or the requisite care is not taken in using a scraper or sanding machine.

One of the most popular methods of removing paint, especially in the painting trade, is to use a blowtorch. This is undoubtedly effective and rapid, but it takes quite a little skill to bake the paint without charring the wood underneath. And it takes a great deal of luck to do the job without setting the house on fire.

In every painted surface in an old house there are joints or cracks, gaps between boards, or between boards and ceiling, or panels and floor. And in every opening there is dust. The walls are full of tinder-like rubbish and nests of mice; stuff that will smolder a long time till a good supply of air gets to it, then, pouf!—and up goes the house. It takes only a lick of the hot flame of a blowtorch to start the smoldering, and no one sees evidences of it until it is too late. When once you have seen a lovely old house burn down because its owner took a chance with a blowtorch, you will never again let one be brought into your house.

The only safe condition under which a blowtorch can be used for paint removal is in working on separate boards, doors, or panels, and preferably in the open. And only the plain white gasoline should be used unless you are immune to lead poisoning! Even under these conditions you need to practice the technique very carefully or you will end up with a piece of wood covered with black splotches where the burns went too deep. And by the time you have removed them there will be none of the original surface left.

The primary rule in using a blowtorch is not to try to take off the full depth of paint at once, and secondly, to keep the flame constantly on the move. The torch works by softening the paint, but the paint quickly hardens again when the heat is removed. The idea, therefore, is to heat a short strip of paint at a time and scrape it off instantly. If you are right-handed you hold the torch in your left hand and sweep the tip of the hot flame over a six- or eight-inch strip of the paint, just slowly enough to make it cockle up without burning or turning black. Immediately you swing the flame well out of the way, so as not to burn either your hand or the work, at the same time scraping off the hot paint with the scraper in your right hand. With a little practice in timing, you can make this quite a rhythmic procedure: burn—scrape —burn—scrape. We have not tried it, but we imagine a metronome would be a big help, or even the right kind of music!

If it is necessary to go over the work twice, as it probably will be, extra care has to be taken with the second burning. The paint is very thin and the wood easily chars. It is then best to whisk the flame only three or four inches at a time and follow it quickly with the scraper. The paint should not, and probably won't, bubble up. But the slightest curling of the surface is an indication that it is soft.

Another danger to be avoided in laying bare the wood is not to dig the scraper into it. The scraper should be narrow, because you heat only a narrow strip at a time, and it should not be too sharp. On the other hand, a fairly stiff blade works best. We have had excellent results with an old $1\frac{1}{2}$-inch chisel, but special precautions have to be taken. Whether you use a scraper or a chisel, the sharp corners should be rounded off on a grindstone or emery wheel. Most of the damage done to the wood by these tools is caused by the sharp corners digging in. The remedy is to remove the corners. Another precaution is to work with the grain as soon as you have found out which way it runs.

Under no circumstances should broken glass be used to scrape off paint. Scratches and gouges show up on bare wood, and no one, however skilled, can manipulate a sharp, uneven edge without marring the surface or tearing off the top fibers of the wood. Stripping down old wood takes time and patience. One way to avoid temptation to haste is to begin the job only when you have plenty of time ahead to give to it. A sloppy job leaves marks for all to see!

Some of the old-time paints leave a very thin, glassy surface on the wood. This is usually a gray or blue-gray color (called buttermilk blue), and it cannot be burned off without damaging the wood. The only way to remove it is to sand it off with very fine sandpaper, taking plenty of time in the process, or to use steel wool together with a good organic paint solvent.

The latest substitute for the blowtorch in removing paint is the infrared bulb. This heats the paint to a fairly high temperature and needs to be handled with care because it, too, can scorch the wood. Apart from being somewhat slower than the torch, and raising the paint in larger areas, it gives comparable results. There is, however, not nearly so much danger of fire because there is no open flame, and no penetrating draft such as a flame produces.

Another paint-removal process that has been popular in the past is the lye bath. Lye is caustic soda and not only eats the paint but burns the wood if it is allowed to go that far. This corrosive chemical is both cheap and fast-working. But for the vertical surfaces which comprise most of the internal woodwork of a house, it is generally more trouble than it is worth. In the first place you need a fairly strong solution, say, a can of lye to two gallons of water—best mixed in a stoneware, enamelware, or iron vessel, never in aluminum.

You cannot use a brush to apply it because it will eat away the bristles. The best tool is an ordinary dish mop with a long, unpainted wooden handle. A good alternative is a small roll of burlap fastened to the end of a stick. With this you apply the chemical to the wall or doorframe, after having donned a pair of rubber gloves. But you can only daub the stuff on so far up the wall. When you get to a height where the mop head is higher than the handle, the liquid runs down your sleeve, burning your arm and eating holes in your clothes. And woe betide you if it splashes! Nothing will destroy the eyesight quicker than a drop of strong lye.

If, after all this, you still persist in going ahead, you will find that frequent applications are necessary, because most of the lye runs down the wall and attacks the floor. This is the reason that the only place to use lye is on horizontal surfaces. Some good, sharp sand sprinkled over the wet surface when you are rubbing more lye on with the mop will help cut into the top layers. The loose paint can be scraped off with a putty knife, and the final remnants washed off with plenty of water and a scrubbing brush. The lye penetrates the wood and, if left there, will not only burn it, but spoil any finish you apply to the wood afterwards. The washing and scrubbing is therefore just as important as taking off the loose paint. In any case the lye will raise the grain and leave a rough surface. Strangely enough, it is less harmful on pine than on oak! This, of course, is because the pine has a closer grain.

A chemical remover that has none of the objections of lye, but several of its own, is the old-style varnish remover. This consists principally of benzol, which, besides being expensive, is highly flammable, and the fumes are dangerous to breathe. Because the benzol vapor is heavy it sinks to the floor and tends to collect in a room. It is therefore essential, if you use it, to have plenty of ventilation, and no cigarettes or matches around. As it is a thin liquid you have to keep swabbing the vertical surfaces so that they remain damp. It works fairly rapidly on varnish coats, but attacks paint very slowly, and successive applications are needed. It may take twenty minutes to half an hour for the surface to become ready for the first scraping. A dull scraper is used for taking off the bulk of the soft paint. The surface is then wiped off with a wad of burlap. After the final scraping the surface should be wet once more with remover and rubbed with steel wool. Thereafter more remover should be applied and the surface wiped off with burlap. This type of remover is slow, and, as will have been gathered from this recital, involves considerable rubbing and scraping. But it does not injure the wood.

## Removers and Refinishers

This brings us to the newest developments in paint removal in which all the virtues of heat, corrosion, and solution are combined but minus their drawbacks. These removers are known as organic solvents. They are composed of various chemicals, but an important ingredient is a substance designed to prevent rapid evaporation of the solvents, so that each application has ample time to do its work before needing renewal.

For house interiors the semipaste type of organic paint remover is best because it contains a high proportion of active ingredients, yet is stiff enough to remain on upright or under surfaces without running or dripping. The one remover of this type with which we have had unqualified success is called Strypeeze. It is unique in that it will remove practically every kind of paint, synthetic or otherwise, including the new resin-emulsion type of water paints. The only coatings it will not take off are casein-based water paints and calcimine. But this is of little importance, for a warm solution of household ammonia will serve for the paint, and whitewash can be sponged off with warm water.

Restorers of antique furniture are particularly partial to it because it contains no strong alkalies or other corrosive chemicals that would damage fine woods. Instead of benzol it contains a less volatile and harmful solvent which is not quite so flammable, though it will burn if you put a light to it. The astonishing thing is that the remover has no ill effects on the skin. You don't have to worry about it getting on your hands or clothes, and it does not injure either the brush you apply it with or the wood you work on. All that you have to do is to float on a heavy coat of the Strypeeze, then wait. The length of time it takes to work depends on the thickness of the paint layer. By checking progress occasionally with a scraper, you can determine when it has penetrated to the wood. At that time you can remove all the paint with a scraper. If the paint coat is thin you can even take it off with a rag or steel wool. A trick you can use on horizontal surfaces is to sprinkle sawdust over the softened paint and roll the whole thing off like pastry.

In dealing with moldings the simplest way is to use steel wool or a

[ 219 ]

soft wire brush. Deep grooves can be cleaned out with a soft-bristle brush dipped in alcohol. You may find that with very thick layers of paint the remover begins to dry before the paint is softened through. In such a case a second coat of remover should be put on top of the first one. If you are not going to repaint the wood you need do nothing more than wipe the surface off with a cloth, though you will probably want to give it a light rub-over with lemon oil. But if you intend to repaint, the surface should be first washed off with alcohol or benzine to remove all traces of wax.

This is the time to do any smoothing off of the wood. Generally size o or oo steel wool will suffice, but surfaces which show signs of shredding may call for size oo or ½ sandpaper. Sanding should always be done parallel with the grain. Sanding across it will leave scratches that are hard to remove. If you are fortunate enough to own a hand-sanding machine of the belt type, this will lighten your labors. But you will have to let the machine support itself by traveling up the surface at a slow rate. The only objection to a machine is that if it slips it may gouge a deep hole before you can stop it. Naturally you should never use anything but the finest sandpaper on a mechanical sander.

## Refinishing

Most old wood, when stripped down by the recommended method without taking off the surface, will have an interesting tone. But very rarely will it have much warmth or depth such as unpainted old wood acquires. Some woods, of course, may not be attractive at all. In soft yellow pine, for instance, or in cypress which shows the light sapwood and dark heartwood, you may have a very light streak of wood next to a very dark one, and the effect is not pleasing. The best results are obtained from a more or less uniform surface pattern, with gentle gradations of shading and no violent contrasts. In other words, the woodwork of a room should constitute a rich but subdued background. This mellow richness is, ordinarily, developed by use and care over many years. In wood that has been covered with paint, this patina can be reproduced only by the application of a penetrating oil or wax and the variations in color toned down by the proper use of stains.

There is, as may be expected, considerable difference between the surface of wood that has been waxed for years and one that has been left in its natural state. In the small houses the raw wood is much more common than the rub-finished surface, but it is extremely difficult to make a surface from which paint has been removed look as though it had never been covered. The cleaned wood usually has a gray cast to it, a "pickled" effect, that wiping over with an oily rag improves but does not entirely cure. What all of this boils down to is that both raw and cleaned wood is improved by the application of wax. If a moderately dull surface is preferred, the wood from which paint has been removed is best treated with a penetrating stain that has wax dissolved in it. When this is thoroughly dried, which will be in twenty-four to forty-eight hours, it can be rubbed to bring out the luster. For a more highly polished surface, which, incidentally we do not recommend, a paste wax can be applied later.

As the paint is cleaned off, the marks that the wood has collected over the years will become more obvious. These, for the most part, will be honorable scars that are evidence of antiquity, and they should not be sanded out. Even a little paint embedded in cracks and corners adds interest to the surface. On the other hand, of course, there may be objectionable stains that are simply ugly. Often these can be removed by one or more applications of oxalic acid, which is an effective bleaching agent. It is made by dissolving two ounces of oxalic-acid crystals in a pint of water. As the stuff is deadly poison, any that is not used should be disposed of at once and not left lying around. The acid solution should be applied with a brush only to the stain and not allowed to spread to the surrounding wood. After a few minutes it should be wiped off to check the color and another coating applied if it is required. When the stain is bleached out, or the area is approximately the same depth of color as the surrounding wood, the acid is wiped off and the area washed with weak ammonia. If this does not work you may have to resort to light sanding or scraping.

Grease spots, which must be removed before staining, are best dissolved out by swabbing with benzine or turpentine. If any part of the wood is badly damaged, it should be replaced by a similar piece of equally old wood, carefully matched as to grain and figuring. If the wood is pine, and an old piece is not available for patching, the new material can be given an antique appearance by washing over with ammonia. Patching should be carefully done by cutting out the damaged part, either in a circle or rectangle, with a drill or fine saw that will not tear the edge of the cut. The patch is cut to size, the edges glued, and tapped into place. When the glue is dry the surface is lightly sanded, and, if necessary, the whole area can be carefully stained to make it an even color.

## *Identifying Woods*

In restoring and refinishing wood surfaces it is very helpful to know with what kind of wood you are dealing. The same treatment given to two different kinds of woods will produce entirely different results. Since the main purpose in applying a transparent surface to wood is primarily to bring out its inherent beauty, the wood must be attractive to begin with. If it is not, we shall either have to cover it with paint or be content with the effects of color and surface finish. The means by which these are developed depend largely upon the texture of the wood to begin with. A porous wood like oak, for example, calls for a method of finishing quite different from that used on white pine which in the raw has very little distinctive grain and is not nearly so porous.

Skill in recognizing the various woods that go into old houses, however, is not something that can be acquired in short order. Neither can it be obtained from books or pictures, for grain is not the only means by which wood is identified and shades of colors cannot be accurately conveyed by the printed word. Color, odor, weight, feel, and other distinctive features all tell their tale to the expert, and the ability to read these signs comes only with practical experience. Even then experts often make mistakes, particularly in dealing with old woods that have changed color with age or have been stained or otherwise finished. We have seen longleaf pine that could hardly be distinguished from oak, birch may look like maple, and cherry like mahogany. Sweet gum is often used with extraordinary success to imitate cherry.

Another handicap to the easy identification of woods is the difference that the method of sawing makes in their appearance. The two ways of cutting a log into boards are to saw the whole thing in parallel slices, or to cut it in four quarters first and saw out boards parallel

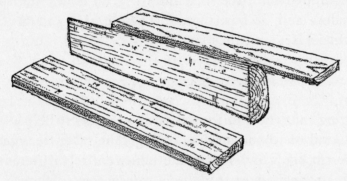

Demonstrating the difference between the grains of plain-sawed and quarter-sawed boards. The plain is at top.

with one of the cut sides. Wood cut by the first method is called plain-sawed, the second, quarter-sawed, and each shows a definite grain pattern very different from the other.

The markings of wood are produced by the long fibers forming the annual rings, and the radial medullary, or pith rays, crossing the rings at right angles. The combination of these is different in almost every wood. In oak, for example, the grain is open, the pores large, and the pith rays so distinct that they are called flakes. In straight-sawed oak these flakes are not usually visible, but they are the most prominent feature of quarter-sawed boards. Such rays, however, are also very plain in sycamore, beech, maple, and cherry, but in chestnut and gum they are very fine. The flakes, therefore, are not alone sufficient to identify any wood. Luckily the woods you are likely to encounter in an old house are few in number. The principal ones will be red and white oak, white pine, yellow pine, chestnut, cedar, and cypress.

White pine, so beloved of the early carpenters, is a soft wood with a close and uniform grain texture, and though it is light in weight it is fairly strong. The color of the new wood is a very pale yellow, and it has few well-defined markings. The old wood is considerably darker on the surface, and even the inside wood often acquires a brownish tinge. The lack of a strong pattern in the grain induces many people to select pieces that show a great many small knots for room paneling that is to be stained. These dark spots certainly give the walls character, but they can hardly be called beautiful. In the old houses such wood was generally covered with paint. Boards that were not to be painted were selected with much greater care!

The terms hardwood and softwood are of little help in classifying the varieties of woods. The term hardwood refers to all broad-leaved trees, and softwood to the conifers (evergreens). But many of the softwoods are actually harder than the hardwoods, and some so-called conifers do not bear cones.

All of which brings us back to the point that wood identification is an accomplishment best learned by actual example. Half an hour spent in a lumber yard or carpenter's shop with an expert will familiarize you with the outstanding differences between the seven commonly used woods. Thereafter frequent handling of the various species of woods will be necessary if you are to become really familiar with their infinite variety and achieve the ability to make a fairly reliable guess.

In restoring or replacing any woodwork it is generally a simple matter to match the existing material as to type. By following the suggestions given earlier regarding sources of materials you may even be able to procure old wood of the kind you need. The simplest way of ensuring that the woods are similar is to compare samples, noting the grain and texture and making due allowances for weathering and finishes that may have been applied as well as the treatment they have received.

In remodeling, of course, the exact matching may not be so important as in restoration, because much larger surface areas will probably be involved. In other words, if you are adding a new room an appearance of age and fitness can be achieved by the proper choice of material and finish without reference to the wood surfaces used elsewhere in the house. There is, in fact, often considerable difference between the woodwork of kitchen and bedrooms and the parlor. Frequently the parlor was improved or elaborated on, particularly in the early 1800s, when fancy fireplaces and mantels became the vogue. Panels were inserted under windows and baseboards were made higher, and ornate moldings added to them. Door and window trim also was made much more elaborate. All of these things can be taken advantage of in making additions.

The same principles, naturally, apply to all remodeling, just as they do in restoration, regardless of the material used. The prime requisite, in all cases, is fitness and suitability. The additions and modifications must be in keeping, not only architecturally but with due regard for the class and style of house. We need to avoid pretentiousness in the small house, and the addition of facilities and appurtenances that properly belong to the mansion. Fancy pergola-type porches and patios of colored flagstone, for example, are entirely out of place on small Colonial houses. Similarly the use of Victorian carriage or hearse lamps to flank the front door are a silly modern conceit that has no place on the dignified small house, or the large one either.

On the other hand, not only permissible but desirable are all the modern conveniences that can be adopted without detracting from the timeless air of the old-time house. With due care all these things can be achieved and the old house made safe, sound, convenient, and economical to maintain and operate without losing its innate charm, if the rules we have discussed in the foregoing pages are applied with discrimination and carried out with taste.

[ 225 ]

# Glossary

ARCHITRAVE—in classical architecture, the lowermost division or an entablature. Any ornamented band or molding carried around a square door or window opening.

ASHLAR—squared and faced building stone. If the sizes of the blocks in a wall varies, it is called random ashlar.

BALUSTER—an upright support of a handrail. "Banister" is a colloquial form of "baluster."

BALUSTRADE—a row of balusters carrying a rail.

BATTEN—a strip of board fastened across two others to hold them together.

BEAD—a convex, rounded molding, usually of semicircular section.

BOLECTION—a molding which projects beyond the general surface of a panel.

BONDING—in bricks or stonework, the binding of the pieces together, by overlapping.

AMERICAN BOND—bricks laid in four or five courses of stretchers to one course of headers.

ENGLISH BOND—bricks laid in alternate courses of headers and stretchers.

FLEMISH BOND—bricks laid in courses of alternate headers and stretchers.

BUTT—(a) the hinged edge of a door; (b) a hinge applied to the edge or butt of a door.

CARRIER—the main support of a stair formed by cutting out a heavy plank for attachment of the treads and risers.

CHAMFER—a bevel formed by cutting away a corner.

CLINCH—to bend over and hammer down the protruding point of a nail so that it cannot be withdrawn.

CLINCHER—a clinched wrought-iron nail.

CORNER BOARD—a vertical board nailed over the corner post of a braced-frame house.

CORBEL—a supporting projection from the face of a wall. Stepped bricks or stones.

COUNTERSINK—to chamfer the edges of a hole so that a screwhead will not project above the surface.

# Glossary

COURSE—a horizontal row of bricks and stones or shingles, etc.

CRADLE—the rubble-filled wood structure that supports a main-floor hearthstone.

DENTIL—a small rectangular block forming one of a series intended for ornament.

DUTCH KICK—the tilt of the eaves in a pitched-roof house typical of Dutch architecture.

DUTCH OVEN—(a) a shallow iron kettle for baking, with tight-fitting rimmed cover to hold burning coals; (b) a tin oven of reflector type for roasting before an open fire.

DOUBLE DOOR—one which is divided into two folds, one of them being hung on each side of a doorway, the two folds meeting at the middle.

ENTABLATURE—the architrave, frieze, and cornice resting on the capitals of columns or analogous parts in post and lintel construction.

ENTASIS—a slight convex curvature given to the taper of a column to make the sides appear as straight lines.

FEATHER EDGE—a board trimmed to a fine edge to fit into a groove in another board.

FENESTRATION—the arrangement and proportioning of windows.

FIRE FRAME—an iron frame set into a fireplace to reduce its size and contain the fire.

FRANKLIN STOVE—a metal fireplace connected to a chimney by a funnel or pipe so as to bring the fire out into the room and conserve heat.

FURRING—a light framework applied to walls, ceilings, floors, etc., to support boards, plaster, or other finish.

FURRING STRIP—any strip used for furring.

GAMBREL ROOF—a form of curb roof, the lower part being at a steeper angle than the upper part.

GEORGIAN—relating to the reign of the four Georges, kings of England—1714 to 1830.

GIRT (or GIRTH)—a horizontal beam framed into the posts of a braced-frame house at floor level; may be front, rear, chimney, cellar, or end girt.

GUDGEON—same as pintle.

HALF-LAPPED—a joint formed by rabbeting two boards so that one overlaps the other.

HEADER—a brick laid so that its shorter face, or head, shows in the surface of a wall.

JOIST—any small timber laid horizontally to support a floor or ceiling.

LINTEL—a horizontal member spanning an opening.

MANTEL—the woodwork around the fireplace.

# Glossary

MORTISE—(a) a rectangular hole into which is fitted a solid piece of the same shape called a tenon, thus forming a mortise-and-tenon joint; (b) a similar hole cut in a door stile to receive a mortise lock.

MULLION—a vertical bar or pier between windows.

MUNTIN—a small, slender mullion forming a sash bar to hold the glass in a window.

PALLADIAN WINDOW—a group of three windows, the center one being higher and having a rounded top.

PEDIMENT—the triangular space forming a roof gable, or a similar form of decoration used over doors, windows, etc. Variations include the scrolled and broken pediments.

PINTLE—an upright pin supporting a hinge, usually with a spike or screw at right angles by which it is attached to a doorframe.

PLATE—the horizontal wooden members that lie on top of a wall or form the topmost horizontal members of a braced frame, and into which the roof rafters are framed.

PORCH—(a) a covered entrance either inside or outside the front door of a house; an entry; (b) any covered enclosure or veranda attached to the house.

PURLIN—a horizontal roof member supporting rafters.

RABBET—a right-angle groove cut in the edge of a board or formed in other materials.

RAKE—the slope of a roof, or the verge board that follows the rake.

RISING HINGE—a butt-type hinge, one half of which moves vertically in relation to the other as it opens.

ROOFTREE—the ridgepole; topmost member of a roof frame.

RUBBLE—rough, broken stone or brick, usually used as filling.

SINK—a recess or depression.

SPLINE (LOOSE TONGUE)—a thin strip of wood placed in the grooves in the edges of two adjoining boards to form a joint.

STILE—an upright piece in framing or paneling.

STRAP HINGE—a hinge composed of two leaves, one made fast to the frame and the other to the door. The common name for a pintle-strap hinge.

STRETCHER—a brick laid lengthwise in a wall.

STRINGER—the side members of a staircase against which the steps abut.

SUMMER—a principal floor timber or beam.

SWAGE BLOCK—a perforated iron or steel block for shaping metal.

TENON—the end of a rail or beam cut to form a projection that may be fitted into a corresponding hole, or mortise, in another piece.

TRAMMEL—an adjustable iron hook for hanging pots over a fire.

TREAD—the flat, horizontal part of a step on which the user treads.

VERGE BOARD—a board or molding covering the end rafter in a gable.

# Bibliography

THE COLONIAL HOUSE—Joseph E. Chandler, Rbt. M. McBride & Co., N.Y., 1924.

DUTCHESS COUNTY DOORWAYS—Helen W. Reynolds, Wm. F. Payson, N.Y., 1931.

DOMESTIC ARCHITECTURE OF THE AMERICAN COLONIES AND THE EARLY REPUBLIC—Fiske Kimball, Chas. Scribner's Sons, N.Y., 1922.

COLONIAL ARCHITECTURE OF CAPE COD, NANTUCKET, AND MARTHA'S VINEYARD—Alfred E. Poor, Wm. Helburn, Inc., N.Y.

THE ARCHITECTURE OF COLONIAL AMERICA—Harold D. Eberlein, Little, Brown & Co., Boston, 1915.

SING, OLD HOUSE—Marion N. Rawson, E. P. Dutton & Co., N.Y., 1934.

AMERICAN HOUSING—Edith A. Allen, Manual Arts Press, Peoria, Ill., 1934.

OLD HOUSES OF NEW ENGLAND—Knowlton Mixer, Macmillan Co., N.Y., 1927.

THE HOMES OF THE PILGRIM FATHERS IN ENGLAND AND AMERICA—Martin Briggs, Oxford University Press, London, 1923.

THE COLONIAL AND FEDERAL HOUSE—Rexford Newcomb, J. B. Lippincott Co., Philadelphia, 1933.

YOUR OWN HOME—Thos. P. Robinson, Viking Press, N.Y., 1941.

HOUSES IN AMERICA—Thos. P. Robinson, Viking Press, N.Y., 1936.

NEW HOMES UNDER OLD ROOFS—Joseph S. Seabury, Fredk. Stokes, 1915.

WHITE PINE MONOGRAPH SERIES—ed. by Russell S. Whitehead, N.Y.

RECLAIMING THE OLD HOUSE—Chas. E. Hooper, Rbt. M. McBride & Co., N.Y., 1913.

MEASURED DRAWINGS OF OLD COLONIAL AND FEDERAL HOUSES—Donald Millar, Architects' League.

MEASURED DRAWINGS OF OLD PHILADELPHIA HOUSES—Donald Millar, Architects' League.

EARLY HOUSES OF OHIO—I. T. Frary, Garrett & Massie, Richmond, Va., 1936.

EARLY AMERICAN DOORWAYS—I. T. Frary, Garrett & Massie, Richmond, Va., 1937.

# Bibliography

EARLY DOMESTIC ARCHITECTURE OF CONNECTICUT—J. Fredk. Kelly, Yale University Press, New Haven, 1924.

HISTORIC HOUSES OF EARLY AMERICA—Elsie Lathrop, Tudor Pub. Co., N.Y., 1941.

EARLY AMERICAN WROUGHT IRON, 3 vols.—Albert H. Sonn, Chas. Scribner's Sons, N.Y., 1928.

EARLY AMERICAN HOUSES—Norman M. Isham, Walpole Society, 1928.

DOMESTIC ARCHITECTURE OF THE EARLY AMERICAN REPUBLIC—the Greek Revival—Howard Major, J. B. Lippincott Co., Philadelphia, 1926.

METROPOLITAN MUSEUM—AMERICAN WING—R. T. H. Halsey & C. O. Cornelius, Metropolitan Museum of Art, N.Y., 1942.

ALBUM OF AMERICAN HISTORY, COLONIAL PERIOD—Jas. T. Adams, Chas. Scribner's Sons, 1944.

HISTORY OF AMERICAN MANUFACTURERS, 3 vols.—J. Leader Bishop, London, 1864.

DICTIONARY OF ARCHITECTURE AND BUILDING, 3 vols.—Russell Sturgis, Macmillan Co., N.Y., 1905.

THE HOMES OF OUR FOREFATHERS—Edwin Whitefield, A. Williams & Co., Boston, 1880.

OLD COLONIAL BRICK HOUSES OF NEW ENGLAND—Rogers & Manson Co., Boston, 1917.

LOST EXAMPLES OF COLONIAL ARCHITECTURE—J. M. Howells, Wm. Helburn Inc., N.Y., 1931.

THE COLONIAL ARCHITECTURE OF MARYLAND, VIRGINIA, AND PENNSYLVANIA—J. E. Chandler, Bates & Guild Co., Boston, 1899.

STORY OF ARCHITECTURE IN AMERICA—T. E. Tallmadge, W. W. Norton & Co., N.Y., 1936.

BUILDING THE DUTCH COLONIAL HOUSE—Aymar Embury, 2d, McBride, Nast & Co., N.Y., 1913.

EARLY AMERICAN DECORATION—Elizabeth Brazer, Pond-Ekberg, Springfield, Mass., 1940.

WOOD FINISHING—F. N. Vanderwalker, Fred. Drake & Co., Chicago, Ill., 1923.

COLOR IN COLONIAL TIMES—M. R. Paul and K. J. Bowman, National Lead Co., N.Y., 1932.

COLONIAL INTERIORS—Leigh French, Jr., Wm. Helburn, Inc., N.Y., 1923.

# Index

# Index

# Index

# Index

# Index

# Index

# Index

# Index

# Index